Jesus 101
God and Man

JOHN L. GRESHAM, PhD

Liguori
LIGUORI, MISSOURI

Imprimi Potest: Thomas D. Picton, C.Ss.R.
Provincial, Denver Province, The Redemptorists

Imprimatur: Most Reverend Robert J. Hermann
Auxiliary Bishop, Archdiocese of St. Louis

Published by Liguori Publications, Liguori, Missouri
To order, call 800-325-9521
www.liguori.org

Library of Congress Cataloging-in-Publication Data

Gresham, John Leroy.
    Jesus 101 : God and man / John L. Gresham. — 1st ed.
      p. cm.
    ISBN 978-0-7648-1931-5
    1. Jesus Christ—History of doctrines. 2. Jesus Christ—Person and offices. 3. Catholic Church—Doctrines. I. Title.
    BT198.G735 2010
    232'.8—dc22

                                                                                    2010011060

Scripture citations are from the New Revised Standard Version of the Bible, copyright 1989 by the Division of Christian Education of the National Council of Churches of Christ in the USA. All rights reserved. Used with permission.

Excerpt from Joseph Cardinal Ratzinger, *Behold the Pierced One: An Approach to a Spiritual Christology*, transl. Graham Harrison (San Francisco, CA: Ignatius Press 1987). © 1986 Ignatius Press, San Francisco. All rights reserved. Used with permission.

Excerpt from Roch Kereszty, "Historical research, theological inquiry, and the reality of Jesus: Reflections on the method of J.P. Meier," *Communio* 19.4 (Winter, 1992) pp. 576-600. © 1992 by *Communio: International Catholic Review*. All rights reserved. Used with permission.

Vatican Council II: Constitutions, Decrees, Declarations. Austin Flannery, ed. Copyright © 1996 by Reverend Austin Flannery, O.P. Costello Publishing Company, Inc. All rights reserved. Used with permission.

English translation of the *Catechism of the Catholic Church* for the United States of America copyright © 1994, United States Catholic Conference, Inc.—Libreria Editrice Vaticana. English translation of the *Catechism of the Catholic Church: Modifications from the Editio Typica* copyright © 1997, United States Catholic Conference, Inc.—Libreria Editrice Vaticana.

Liguori Publications, a nonprofit corporation, is an apostolate of the Redemptorists. To learn more about the Redemptorists, visit Redemptorists.com.

Printed in the United States of America
14 13 12 11 10   5 4 3 2 1
First edition

To Monsignor James P. Callahan
Rev. Christopher M. Martin
Rev. Rodger Fleming

Contents

Foreword

I n *Jesus 101*, Dr. John Gresham, Associate Professor of Systematic Theology at Kenrick-Glennon Seminary, has written a basic introduction to Christology for the average lay reader in the pew. It is well grounded in the scriptural and Catholic understanding of Jesus.

It is written in straightforward, concrete, and inspiring prose. It reveals the Jesus behind the sacraments and alive within the Church and its believers. Written in the simple, yet profound, style of Mother Teresa, this work awakens within us the Jesus for whom our hearts have been hungering and thirsting. It flows from a heart that has been transformed by a personal faith experience of Jesus and from a head that communicates that experience in the context of the Church's universal teachings.

The opening sentence of the first chapter states, "At the heart of Catholic teaching is a person, the person of Jesus Christ."

So many Catholics long to experience in a deeper way the person of Jesus within our teachings and within our worship. When people make this discovery, their lives change dramatically.

While the language is simple, the message is profound and substantive. Take for example the quote from Cardinal Ratzinger's *Behold the Pierced One*: "Since the center of the person of Jesus is prayer, it is essential to participate in his prayer if we are to know and understand Him...." When we apply this to praying the Eucharistic Prayer, the Mass really becomes alive, because we enter into Jesus' prayer to the Father, and that is a powerful experience!

To know the name of a person and his title gives us access to that person. Dr. Gresham explores at least fifteen biblical titles of Jesus, each of which reveals a different charism of the Master.

Checking out a person's resume is a standard practice for choosing friends and employees. The author explores thirteen mysteries in the life of Jesus, which invite us to contemplate Jesus in his unfolding revelation of himself as our Savior and Lord.

In reflecting on the many images of Christ that the Church puts forward for prayerful contemplation, we experience the power and the love of the person of Jesus. Consider, for example, the line, "The crucifix can teach us so much because it reveals the heart of Jesus." So many one-liners in the book could furnish the basis of an extended meditation on the person of Jesus.

I highly recommend *Jesus 101* to anyone who wishes to experience a personal relationship with Jesus and to grow in that relationship through prayer, through the Mass and the sacraments, through Catholic art, and through the teachings of the Catholic Church.

Simply put, this book exudes the richness of the Church's understanding of how to engage the person of Jesus in a way that transforms us. I highly recommend it.

MOST REV. ROBERT J. HERMANN
AUXILIARY BISHOP OF SAINT LOUIS, MO

Introduction

This book is a short introduction to Jesus Christ written from a perspective of faith, hope, and love. First of all, the book is written from a perspective of personal faith in Jesus Christ. I write about Jesus as one who believes in him as the Son of God. When I was sixteen, I first committed my life to Jesus Christ as my Lord and Savior and now that I am in my fifties, he is still the foundation for my life. My conversion to Christ came about through reading the Scriptures. Years of personal and academic study of Scripture since then have only increased my faith in the truth and power of the Bible. Scripture is the written Word of God that through the medium of human words gives witness to the Word Incarnate. This book is based upon a reading of the Scriptures from a perspective of faith in their power to communicate to us the truth about Jesus Christ.

I do not write merely out of my own personal faith in Christ, however. I write from the perspective of Catholic faith, the faith in Jesus Christ handed on by the Church. It was precisely through study of the early Church fathers and the first Church councils that I first discovered tradition as a work of the Holy Spirit in the Church. Reading the writings of the Church Fathers and following the guidance of the early Church councils led me into a deeper understanding of the mystery of Christ revealed in Scripture. That discovery of tradition eventually led me into the Catholic Church. In the teaching of the early Church councils, I discerned the voice of the Spirit. I later discerned that same voice in the teachings of the second Vatican Council and in the *Catechism of the Catholic Church*. This book is informed by the teaching of the Church that guides us into the authentic understanding of the fullness of truth given in Christ and handed on by Scripture and tradition.

Faith is not merely the handing on of doctrines and intellectual concepts. Catholic faith in Jesus Christ is concretely lived by receiving the sacraments and participating in the liturgical and devotional life of the Church. Along with my reading of the Church fathers, the documents of Vatican II and the *Catechism*, it was my experience of Jesus Christ's presence in the holy Eucharist that drew me into the Catholic Church. My knowledge and experience of Jesus Christ has deepened over the years by participation in the sacramental worship of the Catholic Church. That knowledge and experience informs the writing of this book, in which I try to show the connections between Jesus as he is known through Scripture and tradition and as he is experienced in Catholic worship and devotion.

This book is also written in hope. I hope that the Holy Spirit will work through my inadequate words to reveal Christ to each reader and to bring each reader into an encounter with Christ, a living Savior who reaches out to each of us with love and mercy. I encourage each reader to accompany the reading of this book with prayer to the Holy Spirit, asking him to reveal Jesus Christ to you in a deep way.

Finally, this book is written out of love. It is an expression of love for Jesus Christ, our Lord and Savior, the bridegroom of our souls. I hope this little book honors and exalts him and in some way expresses something of the "glory of God in the face of Jesus Christ" (2 Corinthians 4:6). Second, it is written as a service of love to those who read it. I have tried to take some of the theological riches of Scripture, tradition, and Church teaching and to present those treasures in an accessible way to assist each reader in knowing Jesus Christ.

This book is written primarily for Catholics who wish to know more about Jesus Christ in the light of Scripture and Church teaching. I have tried to make it accessible to those without academic training in Scripture or theology. At the same time, I have not tried to "dumb it down," but rather I hope to convey something of the fullness of scriptural and Church teaching on Jesus Christ. In addition to Catholics, I hope other Christians might find this book to be an illuminating Catholic perspective on our shared faith in Jesus Christ. I hope non-Catholic Christians will discover ways in which some of the insights of Catholic faith can help them to know Christ better. Perhaps even non-Christians might find this book helpful, as well. I do not try to argue for the Church's claims about Jesus Christ, so doubters and skeptics will not find answers to all their questions in this book. Yet, they may find it helpful to know something about the content of Catholic belief in Christ. The French Catholic philosopher Blaise Pascal said that we should first help non-believers see the beauty of our teaching and then offer arguments for why it is true. I hope any non-Christians reading this book will catch a glimpse of the beauty of Christ and be encouraged to search further concerning the truth of Christ.

The first chapter begins with an overview of a Catholic approach to Jesus Christ. In this chapter, I try to answer such questions as: What is the role of the Catholic Church in our knowledge of Jesus Christ? What is the Catholic understanding of Christ in Scripture, tradition, and the Eucharist? What is the relation between the Christ of Catholic faith and the Jesus of history? Do Catholics have a personal relationship with Jesus? Chapter 2 digs into Scripture to uncover the meaning of Jesus' names and titles. What is the meaning and theological significance of such names and titles as "Jesus," "Christ," "Lord," "Son of Man," "Son of God," and others? This chapter also speaks of the three messianic offices of Christ as prophet, priest, and king. I will show how each office is foreshadowed in the Old Testament and fulfilled and perfected by Jesus Christ. Chapter 3 provides an overview of the life of Jesus, as revealed in Scripture, read in the light of tradition, with a focus on the theological meaning and significance of each event in his life. The fourth chapter moves from Scripture into the teaching of the early Church fathers to trace how the first ecumenical councils led the Church step by step into a deeper understanding of the mystery of the Person of Christ in his divine and human natures. Our study will take us from the first to the seventh ecumenical councils. That seventh council reaffirmed the Church's practice of venerating images of Christ, and I conclude that chapter with a look at the image of the Sacred Heart, which symbolically summarizes the teaching of these councils. The final chapter will consider the teaching of the Second Vatican Council on Christ, with its emphasis on his continuing ministry through the Church.

The primary sources used in the writing of this book are the Scriptures and the *Catechism of the Catholic Church*. Scripture citations and references to the *Catechism* are cited in parentheses in the text. References to the *Catechism of the Catholic Church* are abbreviated as *CCC* followed by the paragraph number. References to other sources are identified within the text.

I wish to acknowledge and thank those who read these chapters and offered their encouragement and advice: my friend Tim Dallas, who read each chapter and encouraged me along the way; my colleague Dr. Daniel Van Slyke, who read the chapter on the Church Fathers and offered some helpful clarifications; and New Testament scholar Dr. Mark Reasoner, who was particularly helpful in providing additional biblical references. I very much appreciated the Carmelites of the Divine Heart of Jesus, who read these chapters while I taught them a course in Christology, especially Sister Immaculata, for her extremely helpful grammatical and stylistic suggestions. I am very grateful to Deb Meister and Liguori Publications for the invitation to write this book, to Bishop Hermann for his kind foreword, and to Dr. Scott Hahn for taking time in his busy schedule to read the manuscript and offer his recommendation. Finally, I wish to express my gratitude to the administration of Kenrick-Glennon Seminary for the semester sabbatical in which I could devote time to this book.

I wrote this book during a time that Pope Benedict XVI declared as the Year of the Priest. While this book is written for lay people, I wanted to dedicate the book to priests. I have known so many fine priests, including those who first led me and welcomed me into the Catholic Church, the faithful priests I am honored to work with as my colleagues at Kenrick-Glennon Seminary, and the many faith-filled young priests I have had the joy of teaching as seminarians. Of all the fine priests I know, however, I wish to dedicate this book to the faithful priests of my parish. As I wrote about Jesus this year, I grew all the more grateful for the work of these faithful priests who day in and day out proclaim the Gospel of Jesus Christ in their preaching, bring the grace of Jesus Christ through the sacraments they celebrate, and model the example of Jesus Christ by their lives of generous service and love. I dedicate this book in gratitude to the priests of Saint Joseph Parish in Cottleville, Missouri: Monsignor James Callahan, Father Chris Martin, and Father Rodger Fleming.

CHAPTER 1
Jesus, the Heart of Catholic Faith

CATHOLIC FAITH IN JESUS

At the heart of Catholic teaching is a person, the person of Jesus Christ. According to the Catholic faith, Jesus Christ is the eternal Son of God, who became man, who taught us by his words and example, who died for us upon the cross, was raised from death, and now lives forever as God and man—two natures united in one person. The goal of catechesis, the teaching and handing on of the Catholic faith, is to bring others into communion with Jesus, that in union with him, they may know the love of the Father and receive the gift of the Holy Spirit. The person of Jesus Christ brings us into communion with the Holy Trinity. Through Jesus Christ, we come to share in the eternal exchange of love between Father and Son in the Spirit (*Catechism of the Catholic Church* [*CCC* 426]). We come to know the triune God, because the Father sent his eternal divine Son to be born in the world as man, to reveal the fullness of divine truth. The book of Hebrews contrasts Jesus to all those who came before him. God spoke in the past in many ways through many prophets and teachers, but now in the fullness of time, God has spoken by his Son. As divine Son, Jesus is the mediator and fullness of divine revelation (Hebrews 1:1–2, *CCC* 65).

The confession and proclamation of Jesus as Son of God

is at the center of the Catholic Church. When Jesus asks his disciples, "Who do you say that I am?" Simon answers, "You are the Messiah, the Son of the living God." Jesus responds by renaming Simon as Peter, the rock, and declares that it was on this rock that he would build his Church (Matthew 16:15–19). When Jesus names Simon Peter as the rock, he acknowledges both his office as the first pope and his confession of faith (*CCC* 424, 552, 881). The rock of Peter and his confession of faith both point us to Jesus Christ himself as the ultimate foundation stone upon which the Catholic Church is built. Through the ministry of Peter and his successors and the faith that they proclaim, we come to know Jesus as the living stone, rejected by men but chosen as the foundation stone for the new people of God to whom we are united as living stones in his Church (1 Peter 2:4–9, *CCC* 756).

Catholic faith in Jesus Christ is centered in the mystery of the Incarnation. The word "Incarnation" refers to God becoming "flesh." The eternal divine Son assumed our human nature to be born, live, die, and to be raised as the man, Jesus of Nazareth. Jesus Christ is God come in the flesh. Saint Paul speaks of Christ as the glory of God revealed in a human face (2 Corinthians 4:6). Throughout the Old Testament, we encounter the desire to see God—often expressed in prayer to see the face of God—yet, God's face remains hidden. Even Moses, who is described as speaking to God face-to-face, only sees God's glory from behind while hidden in a rock (Exodus 33:11, 18–23). The Old Testament prayer that God will shine his face upon us is answered by the Incarnation. In the face of Jesus, we see God. By looking at his life and hearing his words, we come to know who God is.

In becoming man, Jesus the Son does not only reveal God, he also brings God to humanity. The *Catechism of the Catholic Church* lists four reasons for the Incarnation (*CCC* 456–460). First of all, the Son came to save us. By becoming man, he brings to humanity divine forgiveness, healing, liberation, light, and life. Second, he reveals to us the love of God. Through the Son we come to know the Father and Spirit. We discover the mystery of God as an eternal communion of love. In the Son coming to us as man, we learn of God's great love for humanity. Jesus reveals the heights and depths of this love, a love that does not remain aloof in heaven but fully enters into and shares our human nature and human condition in order to raise us up to share God's life in heaven. This sharing of divine life with humanity is the third reason for the Incarnation. This is what the Church Fathers called the "marvelous exchange" (*CCC* 526). The Son takes what belongs to us, our human nature as well as our burden of sin and death, in order to give to us what belongs to him, divine life and holiness. He became man so that we might become divine. This divinization does not mean that we cease to be human creatures, but by the grace given to us through the Incarnation of Jesus Christ, we come to share in the divine life of God. This divine life is that gift of grace that makes us children of God and transforms us into the image of the Son. The divine image expressed through the humanity of Jesus the Son is the fourth reason for the Incarnation. Jesus restores the divine image to humanity and provides us with a model for authentic and holy human living. We are created in the divine image, but we have wounded and marred that image through sin. Jesus restores the divine image to human nature and lives a life of service to others, which provides us with a model to emulate.

As our model, Jesus shows us the truth about humanity and directs us toward our true destiny as human beings. Vatican II emphasized that "only in the mystery of the Incarnate Word does the mystery of man take on light....Christ the Lord...*fully reveals man to himself* and brings to light his most high calling" (*Gaudium et Spes*, 22). Contemplating the glory of God in the face of Jesus, we may come to know God and, at the same time, come to a deeper understanding and appreciation of our human dignity and ultimate destiny as those beloved by God and called to become his children by our communion with Christ. As human beings, we puzzle over the mystery of our own lives: our origin, our destiny, our sufferings, our sins, our hopes. Jesus comes to reveal the mystery of humanity within the mystery of God's love for us and his gift of redemption. The Church invites us to gaze on the face of Jesus not only to come to understand the mystery of God, but also to understand the mystery of humanity. Jesus teaches us to understand ourselves as created in God's image, wounded by sin, and yet loved by God and embraced by his mercy and called to life and redemption through union with Jesus Christ.

JESUS IN CATHOLIC FAITH

Jesus is at the heart of Catholic doctrine, worship, morality, and prayer. The fullness of truth that the Catholic Church proclaims is rooted in Jesus Christ as the Word of God Incarnate. Through Jesus we come to know God the Father, and from him we receive the Holy Spirit of Truth. The Holy Spirit, the Spirit of God, also known as the Spirit of Christ or the Spirit of the Son, makes Jesus the Son known and unites us to him. All that the Church teaches on the gifts of grace, salvation, and eternal life is the expression of the saving work of Jesus Christ for humanity. The Marian dogmas are all based on the relation of the Blessed Virgin Mary to her son Jesus. Catholic ecclesiology rests on an understanding of the Church as founded by Christ and united to him as his body and bride, carrying on his prophetic, priestly, and royal mission.

When we move from doctrine to worship, we continue to find Jesus Christ at the heart of Catholic faith. Christ is the high priest who reconciles us to the Father (Hebrews 4:14–16, 8:1–2). The ordained priesthood and the common priesthood of all the baptized are two ways of participating in the priesthood of Christ. United to him, the whole Church offers its praises to God in the liturgy of the Church. Jesus Christ is present in the songs and prayers of our worship, in the proclamation of the Word, and above all in the Blessed Sacrament. The sacramental character of Catholic worship is rooted in the mystery of the Incarnation. In the Incarnation, God provided salvation in a visible and tangible way through the flesh of Jesus Christ. By the sacraments, God continues to offer that gift of salvation in visible and tangible ways through water, oil, wine, and bread. In all of the sacraments, Christ is present, and it is his word and power that makes each sacrament efficacious. At the source and summit of Catholic worship is our union with the sacrifice of Christ in the Holy Eucharist. This Christ-centered worship leads to transformed lives. The entire section on Catholic morality in the *Catechism of the Catholic Church* is entitled "Life in Christ" (*CCC* 1691–2557). Through his grace, by our union with Christ, we fulfill the law of God, which is revealed most fully by the example of Christ. The Catholic moral life is rooted in the call to love as Christ loved. Our ability to follow Christ is rooted in the grace given in the sacraments and nourished by prayer.

At the heart of Catholic prayer, we again find Jesus. Jesus teaches us to pray. It is in and through his prayer that we pray to the Father. Our prayer becomes a participation in the eternal dialogue between the Father and the Son. In union with the Son, we pray to the Father, and with the Son, hear the Father speak to us as his beloved children. We pray to Jesus as our Savior, our Lord, our friend. We pray to the Holy Spirit as the one who renews us and enables us to call upon Jesus as Lord and to cry out to God the Father (Romans 8:26–27). In contemplative prayer, we learn to gaze upon the face of Jesus in silence, receiving him as the Word of God and joining in his own ineffable prayer to the Father. The centrality of Jesus in the Catholic prayer is summed up by Saint Augustine, who says that Jesus prays for us as our priest, Jesus prays in us as head of his body the Church and is prayed by us as our God and Lord (*CCC* 2616).

Centered as it is on Jesus, the Catholic faith is not based upon a philosophy or an ethical system. Catholic theology makes use of philosophy and teaches ethics, but those do not provide its ultimate foundation, nor do they express its central content. Catholic faith is rooted in a person and an event. That person is Jesus Christ, and the event is his coming into human history.

JESUS IN HISTORY

At midnight Mass on Christmas Eve, the cantor traditionally sings an announcement of Jesus' birth, which places the event in time, counting the number of years according to Jewish tradition, from the creation of the world, the flood, and such significant dates in salvation history as the birth of Abraham, the exodus from Egypt, and the anointing of David as king. Then the announcement shifts, counting the years from the first Olympic Games in Greece, from the founding of the city of Rome, and from the reign of the first Roman emperor. Regardless of the precise accuracy of the dates, this liturgical announcement emphasizes that this event we celebrate on Christmas, the Incarnation and birth of the divine Son become man, occurs in history. Likewise, in Scripture, Jesus' birth is fixed in history as occurring in the reign of Caesar Augustus, and his death, in both Scripture and the Creed, is dated during Pontius Pilate's rule as Roman governor of the province of Judea. In such ways, Christian faith affirms the very real and particular historicity of Jesus.

Yet it is precisely this historical foundation that is questioned today. A long history of skeptical scholarship and speculation, now popularized by novels and movies, has called into question the historical reliability of the face of Jesus portrayed in the Gospels and Christian tradition. The attempt to excavate the "real" Jesus of history behind the Gospels and Christian tradition has come to be known as the "quest for the historical Jesus." Since the Incarnation is an event in history, Catholic faith is not opposed to the use of historical research to shed light on Jesus Christ. However, Catholic faith would call into question a number of premises that have led many of these questers to skeptical conclusions about the historical Jesus.

First of all, the quest for the historical Jesus presupposes a distinction between Jesus, the man who lived in history, and Jesus as the object of Christian faith portrayed in the Gospels and subsequent Christian tradition. The latter they label the "Christ of faith," which they distinguish from the "historical Jesus." According to those on this quest, the historical man Jesus has been transformed by Christian faith into the divine Son of God. The real Jesus, the merely human Jesus, is somehow hidden underneath that layer of Christian faith and devotion. These questers hold that the historian must critically sift through the New Testament and other early writings about Jesus to identify those sayings and actions that go back to the historical Jesus and separate them from the later layers added by the Church. From a historical perspective, one problem with this approach lies in the very short time period from the life of Jesus to the first Christian writings. It is barely two decades from Jesus to the first letters of Saint Paul, and another few decades to the completion of the canonical Gospels. Some scholars date all the Gospels as written prior to the destruction of Jerusalem in 70 AD (a major historical event that is never mentioned explicitly as a past event anywhere in the New Testament). While scholars debate the precise dates of the Gospels, virtually all of them agree that they are written in the first century. This places these writings mere decades from the events they describe. All are written within the living memory of eyewitnesses to Jesus in the first Christian generation. There is no lengthy historical process by which this man is deified, but only the immediate witness of his followers that this man is Messiah and Lord. Devotion to Jesus as Messiah and divine Lord does not evolve gradually over centuries but explodes suddenly like a religious big bang in the first century.

In addition to this and other historical issues that have been raised against the quest for the historical Jesus, we must add an important theological criticism. The distinction between the Jesus of history and the Christ of faith presupposes that the historical reality of who Jesus really is has been distorted by Christian faith. Admittedly, some questers qualify this by defining "historical Jesus" as the knowledge of Jesus accessible to exclusively historical criteria, but the implication remains that somehow this historically reconstructed Jesus gives us a more accurate and reliable understanding than a view of Jesus informed by faith. However, if Jesus is indeed God Incarnate, then historical criteria alone will never grasp the reality of Jesus. When we encounter Jesus in history, we encounter the mystery of divine self-disclosure, a mystery that can only be grasped by faith. Faith does not distort the reality of Jesus. Faith illumines the reality of Jesus, and only faith enables us to fully understand the history of Jesus in its depth and fullness. Thus, from the Catholic perspective, the historical Jesus "is" the Christ of faith.

Catholic faith identifies the Jesus of history with the Christ of faith because it approaches Jesus from the premise of continuity. The quest for the historical Jesus is based on the premise that there is some discontinuity between the historical Jesus and the faith of the Church. Thus, there is a gap between the historical Jesus and the New Testament writings about Jesus. Catholic faith rejects this premise. The Catholic approach to Jesus believes there is continuity between Jesus, the faith of the early Church, the New Testament writings, and later Christian tradition. This Catholic premise of continuity is rooted in our faith in the Holy Spirit. Jesus promised to send the Holy Spirit to guide the Church into all truth and to bring to remembrance all that he taught (John 14:26, 16:13). Through the illumination of the Holy Spirit, the Church penetrates and grasps the inner divine meaning of all that Jesus said and all that he did (*CCC* 66, 94).

The Catholic approach to Jesus also emphasizes apostolic continuity. This Spirit-led continuity takes historical form through apostolic succession. The apostolic foundation of the Church ensures the continuity from Jesus to early Christian tradition and the New Testament documents. The Twelve Apostles, including Saint Matthias, who was chosen to replace Judas, were those who spent time with Jesus in his public ministry, witnessed his resurrection, and received instruction from the risen Lord prior to his ascension to heaven (Acts 1:1–3). They transmitted what they had learned from Jesus in their preaching and catechesis. The Gospels convey first-century apostolic traditions consigned to writing by the Apostles or their companions and disciples. Then, to ensure the faithful transmission of these teachings, the Apostles appointed bishops in every city to faithfully transmit the truth about Jesus. This process was described in an early Christian letter, written to the Corinthians by Saint Clement of Rome toward the end of the first century. According to Saint Clement's account, the Apostles received the Gospel from Jesus Christ, and as they went forth preaching, they appointed bishops for the believers in each city. The apostolic witness to Jesus Christ is preserved in the Gospels and faithfully handed on to subsequent generations by this succession of bishops.

Today many reject this apostolic witness found within the four canonical Gospels. They appeal to numerous Gospels written much later by second-century dissidents from the apostolic tradition. These so-called Gospels of Mary Magdalene, Thomas, and others—even Judas, the Lord's betrayer—are not

Gospels at all. They do not recount the life of Jesus, but put a second-century heresy called Gnosticism into the mouths of Jesus and his followers. The Gnostics embraced a radical dualism between spirit and matter and rejected the doctrine of the Incarnation. We can respond to these Gospels today, just as Saint Irenaeus did when they were newly published and hot off the press in the second century. As a bishop defending his flock from error, Saint Irenaeus directed his followers away from these spurious writings to the three-fold apostolic foundation of the faith: apostolic writings, apostolic tradition, and apostolic succession. The truth about Jesus, he argued, is known through the apostolic writings consisting of the four Gospels and other New Testament writings, the apostolic rule of faith or tradition summarized in the creedal teachings of the Church, and the apostolic succession represented by the teaching of the bishops who succeeded the Apostles. As in the second century, so today, the Church faithfully transmits the apostolic witness to the truth about Jesus through Scripture, Tradition, and the magisterial teaching of the popes and bishops as successors to Saint Peter and the Apostles.

WHY DID JESUS NOT WRITE A BOOK (BUT STARTED A CHURCH)?

Saint Augustine faced something like a quest for the historical Jesus back when he lived in the fourth century. In the introduction to his "Harmony of the Gospels," Saint Augustine describes some skeptics who rejected the canonical Gospels because they were not written by Jesus himself. They even claimed to have a document written by Jesus to Peter and Paul in which Jesus supposedly explained the "magical" powers by which he worked miracles. Of course, they could not produce such a document. Moreover, they apparently did not know that Paul was only converted after the resurrection and ascension of Jesus and thus could not have been a recipient with Peter of a letter written during Jesus' public ministry. Augustine mocks their ignorance and attributes it to their misinterpretation of paintings that portrayed Peter and Paul as apostolic founders of the Church at Rome. Augustine's mocking rebuke may apply as well to those today who seek to find the secret of Jesus in some DaVinci painting rather than in the teaching of the Gospels!

Others in Augustine's day simply criticized the fact that Jesus wrote no book, hence leaving us to depend on what his disciples said about him. These critics, much like many modern critics, accused the disciples of exaggerated language that transformed Jesus from a wise man into God. Augustine answers them first by noting other esteemed philosophers such as Pythagoras or Socrates who wrote no books. He argues for the veracity of the Gospels based on their fulfillment of Old Testament prophecy and their power as evidenced by the growth and success of the Church in overthrowing pagan polytheism. Then Augustine emphasizes that Jesus did not come simply to impart such wisdom as could be written in a book. Jesus Christ came into the world to bring about something new in human history. As a divine and human mediator, Jesus accomplished redemption in time. As the eternal divine wisdom by which all things were made, he became man to bring to man the gift of wisdom. This wisdom is known only by participation, not by mere reading, but by a sharing in his truth through love given by the Holy Spirit. Prophets before him spoke of his coming by way of prediction. The Apostles after him gave witness to his coming in their preaching and in the Gospels.

Augustine adds the observation that the Apostles wrote as members of Christ's body. Christ the living head of the Church wrote through these members of his Church as his instruments and hands through which he communicates his truth to later generations. So in a sense, Augustine concludes, Jesus did write a book, but he wrote it through the members of his body in the Church he established. Saint Thomas Aquinas, among the hundreds of questions addressed in his *Summa Theologica*, also asks why Jesus did not write a book. Basing his response to the question largely on Augustine's discussion, he picks up on this last point and emphasizes, among his other answers, that the Gospel was transmitted according to Jesus' orderly plan: teaching the disciples and then commissioning and sending them to teach others. A modern Catholic theologian, Father Roch Kereszty, emphasizes the plan of Jesus when he alludes to this question in the article, "Historical Research, Theological Inquiry and the Reality of Jesus," published in the journal *Communio* in 1992. Father Kereszty argues that this plan of Jesus shows that he intended to use the Church, rather than an autobiography, as the means of handing on his memory to others. Father Kereszty concludes:

> *God's intention was to bring about a community of faith around Jesus so that the understanding of Jesus would become inseparable from accepting the witness of this archetypal community...If Jesus wanted to reach all humankind through a community whose faith life and ritual are to continue the faith, life and ritual of this*

archetypal apostolic community, then the fact that Jesus himself authored no book or letter makes complete sense.

Jesus' plan from the beginning was to transmit the memory and knowledge of who he was, not through his own written memoir, but through participation in the Church he founded. Jesus never intended that we would have to go back in the past on a quest to find him through historical investigation. He can be found living today within the Church he founded.

JESUS IN THE CHURCH

The first letter of Saint John begins by referring to the manifestation of Jesus in history as the eternal Word of Life made visible, seen and touched by the Apostles. Saint John proclaims this message to the recipients of his letter and invites them into fellowship. His initial invitation, however, is not to immediate fellowship with Christ or with the Father. Rather, he writes, "What we have seen and heard we proclaim now to you, so that you too may have fellowship with *us*" (1 John 1:3). This "us" refers to Saint John the Apostle and the apostolic community. It is through fellowship with this apostolic community of the Church that one comes to know and understand the mystery of that which the first Apostles saw and touched. Saint John goes on to say, "*our* fellowship is with the Father and his Son Jesus Christ," and he calls his readers into fellowship with God and with one another (1 John 1:3, 6–7). In fellowship with the apostolic community, we come into the fellowship of the Father and the Son. Through the proclamation and sacramental life of the Church, we too see the glory of God revealed in the face of Jesus and receive his life-changing touch.

Holy Mother Church, "pillar and bulwark of the truth," guards the memory of the apostolic witnesses and hands it on to her children (1 Timothy 3:15, *CCC* 171). The Holy Spirit ensures the faithful transmission of the Church's memory in her traditions. Mary, who contemplated the mystery of Jesus in her heart, is a symbol for the maternal memory of the Church. The Church as a community gathered around the Apostles and their successors, imitating Mary as the first disciple and guided by the Holy Spirit, preserves and transmits the truth about Jesus as a living memory. The Church, as body and bride of Christ, is the living subject whose memory of Jesus is transmitted to us by her proclamation and in her sacraments.

THREE KEYS TO THE IDENTITY OF JESUS, TAUGHT BY THE MASS

The Church gives us three keys to understanding the mystery of Jesus Christ. Each key is affirmed by the New Testament, confirmed by Tradition, and embodied in the worship of the Church. The first key to understanding Jesus as taught by the Church is to recognize him as the fulfillment of God's plan for human history. This theme of fulfillment pervades the New Testament and guides the Church's interpretation of the Old Testament. The Church teaches this key in every Mass through the Liturgy of the Word. Readings are usually taken from the Old and New Testaments in order to reveal the pattern in which Christ is prefigured in the Old Testament and the Old Testament is fulfilled in the New Testament (See *CCC* 1093–1095). Based upon Jesus' fulfillment of God's plan revealed in Scripture, the Church learns to interpret all of human history as centered in Jesus. The Church "believes that the key, the center and the purpose of the whole of man's history, is to be found in its Lord and Master" (*CCC* 450). In every Mass, we reflect upon Jesus as the fulfillment of God's plan revealed in the Scriptures, and we are invited to find fulfillment for our own lives within that plan.

The second key to understanding the mystery of Jesus explains the first. How can one human life bring history to its goal? How can one man fulfill every promise of the Old Testament? The answer to these questions is found in the mystery of Jesus' divine origin. He fulfills human history because he is the divine Lord of history, the divine Son of God made man for our salvation. The second key to understanding Jesus is to recognize the mystery of the Incarnation and to confess the secret of Jesus' divine identity. Beginning with Saint Peter's confession of Jesus Christ as the Son of God, the Church has expressed her faith in Jesus' divine identity in the form of professions of faith. As the Church contemplates the person of Jesus revealed in Scripture and responds to challenges to that faith raised by heretical misunderstandings, the Church's own understanding and articulation of the mystery grows. The Church develops a vocabulary of faith expressed in her creeds. By handing on the creeds, the Church teaches the mystery of Jesus' divine personhood, and the faithful are reminded of this key to Jesus' identity every time they profess the Creed in Mass.

The third key to understanding Jesus is to grasp the mystery of his death and resurrection as the means by which he brings God's plan to its fulfillment. Despite Jesus predictions of his death, the Apostles themselves do not fully understand Jesus' mission until that mission is fulfilled by his death and resurrection. After he is raised from death, Jesus upbraids his disciples, "Oh, how foolish you are! How slow of heart to believe all that the prophets spoke! Was it not necessary that the Messiah should suffer these things and enter into his glory?" (Luke 24:25–6). By recording the Apostles' own earlier incomprehension, the Gospels communicate to later generations that the secret to the mystery of Jesus cannot be understood apart from his death and resurrection as the fulfillment of his mission. His own close disciples did not fully understand the mission of Jesus until after he was crucified and raised from the dead. The mystery of his death and resurrection for our salvation remains as a crucial key to knowing Jesus. That is why Saint Paul proclaims Christ crucified as the heart of the Gospel (1 Corinthians 1:23, 2:2). Saint Paul also preaches that if the crucified Lord has not been raised, we are still in our sins and our faith is vain (1 Corinthians 15:14). Only in the light of the resurrection, do we see Jesus' death as victory rather than defeat. To know Jesus, one must come to know him in his dying and rising. This leads Saint Paul to cry out in prayer his desire to know Jesus in the power of his resurrection and the fellowship of his sufferings (Philippians 3:10). Catholic contemplation of Jesus places the death and resurrection at the heart of the mystery of Jesus. Each Mass reminds us of the third essential key, the centrality of Jesus' cross and resurrection, by the sacramental representation of Jesus' sacrifice and the invitation to communion with the risen Lord by sharing in his Body and Blood, which he poured out as his gift to us.

In the Mass, the Church teaches us these three secrets to the identity of Jesus. In the reading and proclamation of the Scriptures, we discover Jesus as the fulfillment of God's plan. In our common confession of the creed, we profess the mystery of Jesus' divine Person in the language of faith handed on by Church tradition. In the eucharistic sacrifice, we come to share in Jesus' death and resurrection as the climax of his mission. We will explore each of these further by considering Jesus in the Scriptures, Jesus in Tradition, and Jesus in the Eucharist.

JESUS IN SCRIPTURE

Throughout the New Testament, Jesus is presented as the fulfillment of the Old Testament Scriptures. In his preaching, Jesus announces that the time for the fulfillment of God's kingdom has arrived with his coming. After his resurrection, Jesus instructs the Apostles and teaches them to understand all the Hebrew Scriptures as finding their fulfillment in him (Luke 24:27, 44–45.). This New Testament theme of fulfillment explains why the Catholic Church includes the Jewish Scriptures in the Christian Bible. When the second century heretic Marcion urged the Church to throw out the Old Testament, he was repudiated. The Catholic Church upholds the Old Testament as part of God's inspired word, alongside the New Testament. The entire Bible is about Jesus Christ. He is prefigured in a veiled manner in the Old Testament and made visible in the New (CCC 129).

Tradition provides a guide to reading the Old Testament in light of its fulfillment through the method of typology. The typological approach reads "God's works of the Old Covenant" as "prefigurations of what he accomplished in the fullness of time in the person of his Incarnate Son" (CCC 128). This typological reading of the Old Testament is based upon the New Testament, which presents numerous figures and events from the history of ancient Israel as "types" that prophetically foreshadow Jesus. In the New Testament, Jesus is presented as the seed of Abraham who brings blessing to all the nations, the New Moses whose law fulfills and surpasses the Torah, the Davidic Messiah who establishes the final, everlasting kingdom. Jesus is the new high priest foreshadowed by Melchizedek, the suffering servant foretold by Isaiah, and the glorious Son of Man from heaven envisioned by Daniel. His death and resurrection fulfill the hopes of Israel in a new exodus, creating a new living temple, in which Jews and gentiles are united as the new covenant people of God. As Saint Paul sums it up, "all" the promises of God find their fulfillment in Jesus (2 Corinthian 1:20). It is not only the history of ancient Israel that reaches its fulfillment in Jesus. By presenting Jesus as the new Adam, Saint Paul emphasizes that Jesus fulfills the history of all humanity. All creation reaches its fulfillment in Jesus. In Jesus, God's eternal plan of love reaches its goal.

While the Old Testament prepares for Jesus' coming, the New Testament announces his arrival and explicates its implications for the Church and all creation. The heart of the New Testament, indeed the heart of all Scripture, is found in the Gospels where we find the life and words of Jesus, the Word Incarnate (*CCC* 125). In Catholic worship, all the Scripture readings lead up to the reading of the Gospel for the day. While lay people may proclaim the readings from the Old Testament and from the New Testament epistles at Mass, the Gospel is proclaimed by a priest or deacon. Those sacramentally configured to the image of Jesus the Incarnate Word, in the person of Jesus the Word, proclaim his words and deeds to us. In honor of that Incarnate Word, we stand for the reading of the Gospel, crossing our forehead, mouth, and heart with a prayer that the

Word might dwell in our minds, be spoken by our lips, and dwell richly within our hearts.

The Church honors the Gospels in her liturgy because it is above all in the Gospels that we come to know Jesus. The Catholic Church "holds firmly that the four Gospels whose historicity she unhesitatingly affirms, faithfully hand on what Jesus, the Son of God, while he lived among men, really did and taught" (*CCC* 126). The Church recognizes that the written Gospels developed through stages but emphasizes that apostolic continuity and the guidance of the Holy Spirit ensure that the truth is faithfully transmitted through each stage. The first stage in the history of the Gospels begins with Jesus himself. The Gospels originate in the life of Jesus, the words he spoke and the deeds he accomplished as witnessed by his chosen Apostles. The second stage is the transmission of his sayings and deeds through the oral teaching of the apostolic Church. Illumined by the light of Jesus' resurrection and guided by the Holy Spirit, the Apostles and other witnesses handed on the truth about Jesus by word of mouth. Then at the third stage, the oral teachings are committed to writing in the four Gospels. Because they author the "Gospel" (the *evangel* in Greek), the four authors are known as the four "evangelists." Each evangelist selects and arranges materials from his oral and written sources according to the particular theological emphases of his Gospel, as he is led by the Holy Spirit. Through all three stages, the process is guided by the Holy Spirit working through apostolic tradition to ensure that the Gospels faithfully hand on the "honest truth about Jesus" (*CCC* 126).

That there are differences between the Gospels is not the discovery of modern critical scholars, but is something the

Church Fathers knew quite well. While some modern scholars find these differences problematic, the Church Fathers saw in the four-fold Gospels a providential blessing that gave us a much fuller portrait of Jesus than any one account could provide. To use a modern analogy, by viewing Jesus from four distinct perspectives, the Gospels give us something like a four dimensional hologram of Jesus. Catholic tradition has associated the distinctive contributions of each Gospel with the four Cherubim hovering around the throne of God in the visions of Ezekiel and the Revelation of Saint John (Ezekiel 1:4–11, 10:14–15; Revelation 4:7). In these visions, four winged, angelic creatures appear, each with a different face: those of a man, a lion, an ox and an eagle. The winged man is typically associated with Matthew who begins his Gospel with Jesus' human genealogy and emphasizes Jesus as royal son of David. Saint Mark is symbolized by the lion. His Gospel begins with a voice crying in the wilderness, like a lion roaring in the desert. (Sometimes, though, it is Matthew who is represented as the kingly lion of the tribe of Judah, and Mark as the humble man or ox who serves.). Saint Luke's Gospel, which emphasizes Jesus as the priestly servant, is usually symbolized by the ox who serves as a humble beast of burden as well as an animal offered in sacrifice. The Gospel of Saint John, which soars on the heights of spiritual contemplation to gaze upon Jesus in his deity as eternal Word and Son of the Father, is almost always associated with the eagle. This four-fold Gospel witness reveals Jesus as the heart of the whole Scriptures and the key to their interpretation. The Church exhorts her members to grow in their knowledge of Jesus through frequent reading of the Scriptures, because "ignorance of the Scriptures is ignorance of Christ"

(*CCC* 133). As Catholics, we read the Scriptures from within the Spirit-led tradition of the Church.

JESUS IN TRADITION

The tradition of the Church both precedes and follows the writings of the New Testament. Prior to the writing of the New Testament, there was already a Church proclaiming, professing, and worshiping Jesus Christ in her sermons, catechesis, creeds, and liturgies. Some creeds and hymns from the Church's early Tradition appear as quotes or allusions in the New Testament. For example, when some members of the Church in Corinth expressed doubts about the resurrection of the body, Saint Paul reminded them of the Creed he had handed on to them from the first Apostles. In 1 Corinthians 15, Saint Paul introduces this Creed by using the language of Tradition: he "delivered/handed on" to them that which he had "received." He then recites this early Christian creed, expressing the Church's faith, "that Christ died for our sins in accordance with the Scriptures, that he was buried, that he was raised on the third day in accordance with the Scriptures, and that he appeared to Cephas, then to the twelve" (1 Corinthians 15:3–5). The repetitive formulaic language of this passage, its departure from Saint Paul's typical style, and the manner in which it is introduced all convince biblical scholars that these few verses are an excerpt from an early creed of the Church. The fact that the creed uses the Aramaic version of Saint Peter's name (Cephas) suggests this creed may date to the very origins of the Church. This creed is significant first of all as a very early witness to the resurrection and secondly as an example of how the Church, from the very beginning, summarized the faith in creedal expressions. This creed provides an early example of the baptismal creeds which continued to develop in the Church and as such could be considered an ancient antecedent to the Apostle's Creed.

Creeds are especially important as a way of expressing belief in Jesus as a divine person. Saint Peter's confession, especially as recounted in Matthew's Gospel, has a creedal quality, "You are the Christ, the Son of the living God" (Matthew 16:16). The account of the conversion of the Ethiopian eunuch in Acts 8, according to some of the ancient manuscripts, has the Ethiopian make the following baptismal confession: "I believe that Jesus Christ is the Son of God" (Acts 8:37). Saint Paul, in a probable reference to a baptismal creed, links salvation to believing in the heart that Jesus is risen and confessing with the mouth that Jesus is Lord (Romans 10:10). In Saint John's letters, the tests of true Christian faith include both love for the brethren and the true confession that Jesus, the Son of the Father, has come in the flesh (1 John 1:23; 4:2, 15; 5:5; 2 John 7). Already, Saint John was responding to those who would deny the mystery of Jesus' divine person and the reality of his Incarnation as true man. These early creedal confessions, cited or alluded to in the New Testament, continue to develop within the tradition of the Church as a means of handing on the apostolic witness to Jesus Christ.

Thus, when the bishops of the Church gathered in the city of Nicaea in 325 to address challenges to the deity of Christ, they followed a long precedence by composing a creed that professed the common faith of the Church. This Nicene Creed, not only handed on the apostolic faith, but it also further developed the Church's understanding and articulation of that

faith. Contemplating the face of Jesus in Scripture, responding to new questions and challenges, the Church grows in her
insight and understanding of that fullness of truth Incarnate
in Jesus Christ (CCC 66, 94). When faced by challenges to her
understanding of the mystery of the Incarnation, the Church
is forced to respond with a clearer articulation of faith. In the
first millennium, the Church responded to such challenges in
a number of ecumenical councils. (An "ecumenical" council
means a council of the "whole" Catholic Church.) Gathered together in the name of Jesus Christ in these Church councils,
the bishops as successors to the Apostles are guided by the Holy
Spirit into a deeper understanding of the mystery of Christ. We
continue to learn from these councils about the mystery of Jesus and how to avoid heretical distortions of the faith. In these
councils, we can discern the Holy Spirit leading the Church
step by step toward a fuller understanding of the mystery of
Jesus Christ. The first ecumenical council of Nicaea (325) affirmed the full deity of Christ. When a new heresy emerged
that questioned the humanity of Jesus, the second ecumenical
council, in Constantinople (381), affirmed his full humanity.
Having affirmed that Jesus was both divine and human, the
third ecumenical council in Ephesus (431) affirmed the unity of humanity and deity in the Person of Christ. Chalcedon
(451), the fourth ecumenical council, summed up the teaching
of the previous councils in its affirmation of the two natures of
Christ (CCC 464–469).

These early ecumenical councils provide the Church with a
lasting vocabulary of faith to express the mystery of Jesus in order to evangelize seekers, refute heretics, catechize the faithful,
and to give praise and adoration to Christ. Catholic faith sees

these Church councils as the work of the Holy Spirit guiding the developing tradition of the Church more and more deeply into the knowledge of Jesus Christ. Sacred Tradition is not opposed to Scripture, nor does the language of the creeds and councils obscure Scripture. Rather, Tradition points us to the mystery of Jesus Christ at the heart of Scripture. Confessing the mystery of the person of Christ in the language given to us by Tradition in the Creed prepares us to receive Jesus in the Eucharist.

JESUS IN THE EUCHARIST

The death and resurrection of Jesus occur as real events in human history. Yet, unlike other events in history, this event does not remain in the past. The Person who dies and is raised is the divine Son of the Father, who with the Father is Lord of time and eternity. His death and resurrection are the fulfillment of the divine plan for all of human history. This historic event has a divine and eternal dimension. At this moment of history, God acts to redeem from death all people throughout history and to offer the gift of eternal life through communion with his Son and through the gift of the Spirit. When we recognize Jesus as the fulfillment of God's plan for human history, when we consider the mystery of his divine person, when we consider his death and resurrection as the moment in which the divine Son gives himself in a human way to every human person, we begin to grasp how this historical event opens itself to all times and draws all times toward eternity.

> *When his hour comes, he lives out the unique event of history that does not pass away: Jesus dies, is buried,*

rises from the dead, and is seated at the right hand of the Father "once for all." His Paschal mystery is a real event that occurred in our history, but it is unique: all other historical events happen once, and then they pass away, swallowed up in the past. The Paschal mystery of Christ, by contrast, cannot remain only in the past, because by his death he destroyed death, and all that Christ is—all that he did and suffered for all men—participates in the divine eternity and so transcends all times while being made present in them all. The event of the cross and resurrection abides and draws everything toward life (CCC 1085).

This is where the Catholic approach differs radically from the quest for the historical Jesus. For those who seek him in the past, this man of Nazareth, like all others who have lived in history, remains in the past. They believe that the details of his life must be retrieved through careful and critical historical investigation in order to reconstruct the meaning of that life among other past events of history. By contrast, Catholic faith proclaims that Jesus is risen! His life is not over. That life is not lost in the past awaiting retrieval by the historian. Jesus' death did not mark the end of his life but rather the culmination of his mission. The cross is the moment in history in which God's saving gift is given for each and every person throughout human history. Risen from the dead, Jesus now offers to each and every person the opportunity to share in this event by which we are saved from death and raised to new life.

It is primarily through the liturgy, by participating in the sacraments and prayer of the Church, that we become contemporaries of Jesus. In liturgical prayer we participate in Jesus' own prayer. Before he became Pope Benedict, Cardinal Ratz-inger responded to the quest for the historical Jesus in an essay entitled, "Taking Bearings in Christology," later published by Ignatius Press in *Behold the Pierced One*. This essay present-ed the prayer of Jesus as the key to historical, theological, and spiritual understanding. The future pope emphasized in that essay that Jesus' whole life was a loving prayer to the Father. We can only come to understand him in light of this prayer. From Jesus' prayer, we understand how he fulfills history in loving obedience to the Father's plan. His intimate conversa-tion with the Father reveals the mystery of his Person as the unique Son who shares in the divine nature of his Father. Jesus' dying prayer from the cross teaches us to understand the mys-tery of his death and resurrection as the Father's gift to us and our gift to the Father. To grasp these mysteries it is essential to enter into and share in Jesus' prayer as the necessary precondi-tion to understanding him. In this essay, Cardinal Ratzinger asserted the following thesis:

Since the center of the person of Jesus is prayer, it is essential to participate in his prayer if we are to know and understand Him...[Participation in his prayer] is not some kind of pious supplement to reading the Gospels...it is the basic precondition of real understanding.

This prayer, the essay continues, occurs in the fellowship of Jesus' followers, within the community of the Church Jesus founded.

The *Catechism* describes the liturgy as "a participation in Christ's own prayer addressed to the Father in the Holy Spirit"

(*CCC* 1073. By liturgical prayer, we are catechized and initiated into the mystery of Jesus (*CCC* 1075). Through the Holy Spirit, in the liturgy and sacraments of the Church, we are united in Jesus' prayer to the Father and we recall, celebrate, and share in the mystery of Jesus and the saving events of his life as present realities (*CCC* 1088, 1104, 1115). All liturgical prayer, as well as all other sacraments, are oriented toward the sacrament of the Eucharist, the "source and summit" of the whole Christian life, for "in the Blessed Eucharist is contained the whole spiritual good of the Church, namely Christ himself." The holy sacrifice of the Mass makes present the one sacrifice of Christ our savior, to which we join our own sacrifice of praise and thanksgiving (*CCC* 1325, 1330).

We prepare for meeting Jesus in the Eucharist and other sacraments of the Church and we respond to that meeting by a life of personal prayer in which we continuously unite our hearts to the heart of Jesus. That prayer then fosters a life in which we come to know Jesus by uniting ourselves to him in service to others. It is not by historical retrieval but by participation in the life of the Church, that the historical and eternal, the human and divine Lord Jesus Christ encounters us in a contemporary, personal encounter.

JESUS IN OUR HEARTS

Evangelical Protestants will sometimes ask us Catholics, "Do you have a personal relationship to Jesus?" As Catholics we should be able to reply to such a question with an enthusiastic, "Yes!" For an Evangelical Protestant, the personal relationship with Jesus often begins by going forward in a church service or revival meeting to ask Jesus into his or her heart. This invitation to come forward and accept Jesus is known as an "altar call." (Most Protestant churches do not have an altar, but they call it an altar call anyway.) So if a Protestant asks if you have a personal relationship with Jesus, he is often asking if you have gone forward in response to an altar call to receive Jesus into your heart. We can assure our Protestant brother that every Catholic Mass has an altar call. Every time we go to Mass, we are given an invitation to come forward and receive Jesus. The entire liturgy has prepared us to receive the Lord Jesus into our hearts and into our very bodies. We have heard his word, read and proclaimed. We have confessed our faith in Jesus in the Creed. The priest proclaims Jesus' death and resurrection, not only in words, but also in dramatic, symbolic actions that recall Jesus' offering of his Body and Blood for us. Through the words of Christ and the power of the Holy Spirit, Jesus' sacrifice, his Body and Blood, become truly present. We prepare to receive him in humble prayers acknowledging our need for salvation and our unworthiness to receive such a great gift: "Lord I am not worthy to receive you...Lamb of God...have mercy on me...grant me peace." And then we answer the invitation. We go forward to receive Jesus as our personal Lord and Savior. But we do not receive him in an exclusively spiritual sense, into our mind and soul. We receive that and much more. Jesus who was Incarnate, who was made flesh for our salvation, who poured himself out and gave himself to us physically and bodily on the cross, continues to give his body and his blood. We receive Jesus into our bodies. Unlike the Evangelical Protestant altar call, which is typically a once-in-a-lifetime event, the Catholic Church calls us to the altar again and again. Every week, every day if we wish, we renew our relationship to Jesus by receiving him afresh. Why must we receive Jesus again and again? Our relationship to Jesus is like a marriage. A healthy marriage is much more than one walk down the altar to say, "I do." As a husband and wife receive one another and express their love for one another again and again, even so do we renew our relationship to Jesus again and again.

While Jesus offers us this incomparable relationship to him in the Mass and the other sacraments of the Church, it is possible to be a Catholic, to go through the motions, and never experience this personal relationship with Jesus. This relationship requires conversion. For the Catholic, conversion is not just a one time event, for we are called to a live of continued conversion in our relationship to Jesus. Conversion means turning away from sin and turning to Christ in faith. The first step toward a more personal relationship to Jesus can begin as simply as praying, "Jesus I am sorry for my sins. I receive you as my savior. I surrender to you as my Lord." The next step is to follow up this personal prayer with a trip to the confessional where Jesus waits to offer his healing grace in the sacrament of penance. This sacrament, which we know by such names as confession, penance, or reconciliation, has another name in the *Catechism* that is seldom used. It is also known as the sacrament of "conversion" (*CCC* 1423). It makes Jesus' call to conversion and the grace of conversion sacramentally present. This sacrament is a personal encounter with Jesus. It is Jesus who hears our confession and forgives our sin, but he makes that forgiveness tangible and present to us, by using the priest to speak, as Jesus' own sacramental representative, those words of forgiveness into our ears. Jesus himself gives us the grace of conversion through the gift of the Holy Spirit. The third step toward a more personal relationship to Jesus is to open oneself to the gift of the Holy Spirit given to us in baptism and confirmation. It is by the Holy Spirit that we are able to confess Jesus as Lord (1 Corinthians 12:3, *CCC* 455). The source of new life in Christ is the love of God poured into our hearts by the power of the Holy Spirit. The Spirit draws us to Jesus, opens our hearts and minds to his word, unites us to his death and resurrection, and brings us into the communion of the Holy Trinity. Through the sacraments, Jesus pours out the Holy Spirit to heal and nourish us and to bear fruit in our lives. The Holy Spirit helps us to pray, even when we do not know how to pray (Romans 8:26–27, *CCC* 735–740). As we open our hearts to the Holy Spirit and let him lead us in prayer, he will lead us to a deeper, personal relationship with Jesus.

JESUS IN OTHERS

As Catholics, we believe in a relationship to Jesus that is personal but not individualistic. Jesus came into this world not only to reconcile us to God, but also to reconcile us to one another. Jesus is sent into the world to gather all peoples, uniting them as many members into his one body (Ephesians 2:13–18; *CCC* 775, 831). We are like many living stones built together into his body the Church, a living temple of the Holy Spirit, built upon the foundation stones laid by the Apostles and prophets upon the chief cornerstone Jesus Christ (Ephesians 2:19–22, 1 Peter 2:4–10). When we come into a relationship with Jesus, he puts us into relationship with others in the Church. This begins with our relationship to the priest and people of our parish. As members of the parish, we also belong to the diocese shepherded by the local bishop standing in succession to the

Apostles. As members of the Catholic Church, we are joined in Christ to the Church universal with a relation to the pope as successor to Peter and pastor of the universal Church. But it is not only those living members of the Church to whom we are related. Jesus unites heaven and earth, so that those here on earth are united to the saints and angels in heaven as well as the souls in purgatory. All are united in one body in Christ (Ephesians 1:10, *CCC* 962). Jesus brings us into the communion of saints. Our brothers and sisters in heaven, by their examples and by their prayers, assist us in following Jesus. Among the saints, Jesus gives us a special relationship to his own mother (John 19:26–27). We pray for our departed loved ones, knowing that even death cannot sever the unity we share with them in the body of Christ. United to Jesus, our relationship to others extends beyond the Church. Jesus says that whatever we do for those who are in need, we do for him (Matthew 25:34–40). From this we are taught as Catholics to find the face of Jesus in the poor and suffering. The personal relationship we have with Jesus transforms our relationships to all our neighbors. By coming to know the heart of Jesus, our hearts will be transformed to love others as he loves us.

CHAPTER 2
The Names and
Titles of Jesus in Scripture

JESUS

An angel instructed Saint Joseph to name the child entrusted to him "Jesus." The name is a contraction of "Yahweh Saves." As the angel explains to Joseph, the child is to be given this name because he is destined to save his people from their sins (Matthew 1:21). While not an uncommon name among Jews of that era, "Jesus" has immense theological significance when applied to this child born in Bethlehem. Biblical names frequently bear theological significance. When God calls the nomad Abram into a covenant relationship and promises to make him the father of many nations, he changes his name to Abraham "father of a multitude." When Jesus calls the Apostle Simon to be the rock on which he builds his Church, he changes his name to "Rock" (*Petros* in Greek or *Cephas* in Aramaic). And so we now know him as Saint Peter.

Of all biblical names, the most significant is the revelation of the name of God. Speaking to Moses from the burning bush, when asked his name, God declares, "I Am that I Am" (Exodus 3:14). In this divine manifestation, God reveals to Israel his sacred name of "Yahweh." So sacred is this name, the ancient Jews would not utter it aloud but rather substituted the word

"Adonai" for the divine name. This name expresses the absolute transcendence of God as he who is the fullness and perfection of being, standing above and beyond all that is created. Yet, in giving this name to Israel, the transcendent God shows his desire to come close and to be present to his creation, to be known and called upon by this name. He first begins to fulfill this desire by giving his name to his chosen people Israel in order that they might be a light to the nations through whom the name of God might be known by all. Thus, the Jewish prophets speak of a day when all nations will call upon the name of Yahweh, acknowledge him as Lord and God, and bow their knee before him (Isaiah 2:2–5, 42:6, 49:1–6, 66:18–23; Zechariah 8:22–23).

These prophecies are fulfilled by the name of Jesus. On the day of Pentecost, Saint Peter recalls the prophecy of Joel, that when the Spirit is poured out, all will call upon the name of Yahweh for salvation. But Saint Peter applies the prophecy to the name of "Jesus" and encourages his listeners to call upon the name of Jesus for salvation (Acts 2:21, 4:12). Similarly, Saint Paul quotes an early Christian hymn that takes Isaiah's prophecy of all nations bowing the knee before the name of Yahweh and applies it to Jesus, proclaiming in song that every knee will bow at the name of Jesus (Isaiah 45:22–24, Philippians 2:10).

Jesus' name is literally a contraction of "Yahweh Saves," and contains the name of Yahweh. By calling on the name of Jesus, we call on the name of Yahweh. The inaccessible name that could not be uttered can now be uttered again and again, as part of the name of Jesus. It is through this name of Jesus, that Yahweh, the transcendent God, has made himself accessible to humanity. As the *Catechism of the Catholic Church* says, "The divine name may not be spoken by human lips, but by assuming our humanity, the Word of God hands it over to us and we can invoke it: 'Jesus,' 'Yahweh saves'" (*CCC* 2666). Thus, Saint Matthew relates the name of Jesus to another name, Immanuel, which means "God with us" (Matthew 1:23). The name Jesus means that Yahweh has come to be with us in and through the child born at Bethlehem.

I AM

Jesus' identification with Yahweh is further emphasized in the Gospel of John, by the use of the "I am" formula. As we have seen, God's name revealed to Moses can be literally rendered as "I am." Moreover, the Old Testament uses the formula, "I am he" to express the identity of Yahweh as the one true God. In the Gospel of John, Jesus frequently uses this divine formula when speaking of himself. On a number of occasions, he uses "I am" followed by a predicate noun to convey divine attributes. Jesus says, for example, "I am the life...I am the truth...I am the light" (John 8:12, 14:6). More significantly, Jesus sometimes simply uses the "I am" formula in an absolute form. Thus, when asked if he thinks he is greater than Abraham, Jesus replies, "Before Abraham was, I am" (John 8:58). These opponents immediately seek to stone him for this comment, which would be blasphemous if spoken by anyone but God. On another occasion, when the soldiers come to the garden of Gethsemane seeking Jesus of Nazareth, Jesus replies "I am" (John 18:5). Most translations render this reply in the more grammatical English, "I am he," but the text is literally, "I am." Those soldiers understood better than some of our modern translators, for they immediately fell to the ground at this utterance of the divine name (John 18:6).

LORD

Jesus' identity with Yahweh, the God of Israel and Creator of the world, is most consistently expressed by the divine title, Lord. Salvation is promised to those who believe in their hearts that Jesus has risen from the dead and confess with their mouth that "Jesus Christ is Lord" (Romans 10:9–13). One of the earliest Christian confessions is this declaration that "Jesus is Lord." Just how early the first Christians began to call upon Jesus and to worship him as Lord is shown by the preservation of an early Christian prayer in Aramaic, the language spoken by Jesus and his first disciples. In his closing comments in the First Letter to the Corinthians, Saint Paul inserts the Aramaic phrase, "maranatha," which means "O Lord Come" (1 Corinthians 16:22). Saint Paul is writing in Greek to a Greek-speaking, predominately gentile church in Corinth, yet he uses this Aramaic phrase without translation. The Corinthians most likely knew this phrase the same way we may know that the Greek phrase *Kyrie eleison* means "Lord have mercy," or the Latin phrase, *Agnus Dei*, means "Lamb of God." These Greek-speaking Christians had preserved in their liturgy an Aramaic phrase from the Church's origins. Thus, Saint Paul preserves for us a liturgical phrase that takes us back to the very beginnings of the Church when Aramaic-speaking Jewish converts to Christian faith were already praying to Jesus as Lord in their worship.

This is all the more significant in light of the ancient Jewish practice of using the word "Lord" as a substitute for the divine name of Yahweh. When Jews came upon the divine name in their reading of the Scriptures, instead of saying it aloud, they would substitute the Hebrew word *Adonai,* which means

"Lord." By the time of Jesus, Jews were dispersed throughout the Roman Empire where they would speak Greek, the international language of the day. (Later, Latin would supplant Greek as the language of the western part of the empire.) To meet the needs of these dispersed Greek-speaking Jews, their Hebrew Scriptures were translated into Greek. It was this Greek version of the Jewish Scriptures, known today as the *Septuagint*, which became the Old Testament used by the writers of the New Testament and the Church Fathers. In the Greek Old Testament, the divine name of Yahweh is typically replaced by the Greek word *Kyrios*, which means "Lord." This term *Kyrios*/Lord is taken directly from the *Septuagint* and applied to Jesus in the New Testament. In fact, a great many of the references to Jesus as Lord in the New Testament are citations or allusions to Old Testament passages about Yahweh, which are now attributed specifically and directly to Jesus. Passages in the Old Testament that speak about Yahweh, the Lord of Israel, are quoted in the New Testament as referring to the Lord Jesus. For example, the phrase, "Day of the Lord," Yahweh's final triumph over evil prophesied in the Old Testament, becomes in the New Testament the day of the Lord Jesus Christ's second coming as judge (2 Thessalonians 2:2). The phrase, "Word of the Lord," which described Yahweh's prophetic word in the Old Testament, refers in the New Testament to the Gospel of Jesus Christ (Acts 8:25).

This identification of Jesus as Lord leads to an early Christian transformation of the Jewish confession of the one God. Devout Jews would daily recite, "The Lord is our God, the Lord is One" (Deuteronomy 6:4). Over and against pagan polytheism, the Jews confessed their faith in the one God from whom and through whom all else is created. Saint Paul cites an early

Christian modification of this Jewish confession which associates the word "God" (*theos*) with the Father, and the word "Lord" (*kyrios*) with Jesus, thereby including both God the Father and Jesus the Son within a confession of divine unity. Contrary to the many gods and lords of pagan polytheism, Christians confess that "For us there is one God, the Father, from whom are all things and for whom we exist, and one Lord Jesus Christ, through whom are all things and through whom we exist" (1 Corinthians 8:5–6).

Through this vocabulary, the New Testament begins to convey the mystery of the Trinity. In the New Testament, the term "God" usually refers to the Father; the word "Lord" usually refers to Jesus the Son. Both, together with the Spirit, share the attributes and identity of the one God who created the world and revealed himself to Israel as Yahweh. In the first exodus, God liberated a people from slavery and revealed his name as Yahweh. This name expresses "what" God is as the "I Am," the being from whom all other existence is derived. In the new and final exodus, God acts through the death and resurrection of Christ to liberate all mankind from slavery to sin and death and reveals his name as Father, Son, and Holy Spirit. This name reveals "who" God is as an eternal communion of love. Saint Paul closes the second letter to the Corinthians with a threefold, Trinitarian divine blessing, which continues to be used in the liturgy of the Church: "The grace of the Lord Jesus, the love of God and the fellowship of the Spirit be with you all" (2 Corinthians 13:13).

The title "Lord" not only describes Jesus' identity as God, but it also says something about our relationship to him. Because Jesus is Lord, we are his servants, literally in the Greek, his "slaves." We owe him our complete and total devotion and allegiance. Because he is the Lord, Jesus calls his disciples to forsake all and follow him. The Lordship of Christ also means that he claims our allegiance before all other earthly obligations. Those who follow Jesus the Lord must even forsake family if they stand opposed to the faith. While Christians honor legitimate political authority, when the state persecutes the faithful or opposes God's laws, the Christian must acknowledge Jesus' higher authority as Lord. The Roman emperors called themselves Lord, and many Christians became martyrs for the confession that it is not the emperor but Jesus Christ who is Lord.

The Lordship of Jesus also transforms our relations to others. Saint Paul declares that as servant of the Lord Jesus, he is called to be a servant to others (1 Corinthians 9:19). The Lord himself set the example by humbling himself to be a servant, washing the feet of his disciples (John 13:12–17). We are called to imitate our Lord in service to others. Jesus is the Lord, in the very form of God, who humbles himself to take on the form of a servant, becoming man, sharing our nature, humbling himself to his death on the cross for us. It is now as the one who was crucified and risen that Jesus is exalted as Lord and worshiped (Philippians 2:5–11). Jesus is honored as the Lord who has faithfully fulfilled his messianic mission as man. That mission is expressed in a particular way by the title "Christ."

CHRIST

"Christ" is not the last name of Jesus, although, as we shall see, it comes to be used as his name. It is originally a title that expresses the office Jesus fulfills in his messianic mission. The word "Christ" is from the Greek *Christos* and literally means "anointed one." It is taken from the Greek word for anointing with oil. The "chrism" oil used in baptism and confirmation derives its name from this same Greek root. The Greek *Christos* translates the Hebrew term for the anointed one, *Messiah*. In ancient Israel, the term "Messiah" refers to anointed kings or priests, or on occasion, prophets. In time, the word comes to refer to a future ideal king, whom God will send to save his people, the coming Messiah for whom Israel awaits.

At the time of Jesus, there are a variety of messianic expectations among the Jewish people as expressed in the Scriptures and other ancient Jewish writings. Some hope for a military king who will overthrow the Romans and restore the political fortunes of Israel. Some look for a messianic priest who will reform and renew temple worship. Others expect a "prophet-like Moses" who will once again feed his people in the wilderness and reestablish God's law through a new and lasting covenant. Some of these prophecies and expectations look for the messianic blessings to extend beyond Israel through the gathering of the gentiles into the promises of God. Some prophecies speak of this coming messianic age as a new exodus in which God will act in history to save his people in a display of divine mercy and power that will surpass his former works. Some even use the language of new creation and hope for a new world in which nature itself will be healed from the effects of sin. While many look for a human Messiah to usher in this age of salvation, others expect a cosmic figure from heaven and still others expect God himself to come and bring salvation. The early Christians saw Jesus as the fulfillment of all these prophecies. The Apostles are taught by the risen Lord Jesus himself, who opens their minds to understand the Old Testament Scriptures in order to see how the messianic prophecies are fulfilled by his coming (Luke 24:44–45). As "Christ" and "Messiah," Jesus is the anointed prophet, priest, and king who fulfills all the promises of a messianic mediator. Because he is God come in the flesh, Jesus also fulfills all those promises that God himself will come to bring salvation.

Jesus' person and office—his name and titles—are so united that "Christ" comes to express not only *what* Jesus does in his messianic office, but also *who* he is as the divine and human one who fulfills those offices. Thus, in the New Testament, the title "Christ" already functions as a name, used interchangeably or in combination with "Jesus." In the New Testament, "Jesus," "Christ," "Jesus Christ," and "Christ Jesus" are all used as his name. Christian tradition continues the New Testament pattern, honoring "Jesus Christ" as the sacred name of our Lord and savior. Ancient Christian scribes inscribe this sacred name in a special way, reminiscent of Jewish regard for the holy name of God. In the liturgy, the celebrants bow at each mention of Jesus Christ's sacred name. The name itself expresses all that Jesus is and does for our salvation, and the repetition of the name, as in the practice of the Jesus prayer, becomes a profound and life transforming experience: "Lord Jesus Christ, have mercy on me a sinner" (*CCC* 2666–2668).

As noted above, Jesus' messianic mission combines the three anointed offices of prophet, priest, and king (revealer, redeemer, and ruler). The office of prophet represents God to the people as revealer, as one who speaks to the people on God's behalf, bearing and transmitting the word of God. Jesus fulfills and surpasses the office of prophet, for he not only bears the word of God, he is the eternal Word of God made flesh. Jesus brings the fullness of divine revelation. The office of priest represents the people before God, offering sacrifice and intercession on their behalf as a mediator of redemption and reconciliation. The priest speaks to God on behalf of the people. As divine and human mediator, Jesus fulfills and surpasses the office of priest by offering himself to the Father for the eternal redemption and reconciliation of the world. The office of the king represents God's rule over the people. Jesus fulfills and surpasses this office by establishing the kingdom of God on earth, which will grow into the everlasting kingdom of heaven. Each of Jesus' messianic offices is foreshadowed by figures in the Old Testament who serve as prophetic types of the coming Messiah. As the prophet like Moses, the priest according to the order of Melchizedek and the royal Son of David, Jesus fulfills the prophetic, priestly and kingly offices of the Messiah. We will discuss each of these Old Testament types and offices and their fulfillment by Christ in what follows but we must first comment on the surprising way in which Jesus fulfills his messianic mission. Jesus' messianic mission reaches its climax in the cross. The cross becomes the pulpit from which Jesus the prophet reveals the depths of divine love; the cross becomes the altar upon which Jesus the priest offers himself as the sacrifice for our sins; the cross become the throne from which Jesus the king rules over our hearts. It is only in the light of his resurrection, that the cross of Jesus can be seen as the place of his messianic triumph as prophet, priest, and king.

THE NEW MOSES

Moses is the first, greatest, and prototypical prophet for all who follow in his footsteps as those called to speak on God's behalf. Today, we usually associate prophecy with predicting the future, but the Old Testament prophets are less foretellers than "forth-tellers." While they speak of God's actions to come in the future, their primary role is to speak God's word to the people in the present, calling them to faithful observance of the covenant within the context of their current situation. The prophets call people back to that covenant given through the first prophet Moses. While Moses is considered the greatest prophet, as the one through whom God revealed the Sinai covenant, the book of Deuteronomy speaks of another prophet to come and the later prophets speak of a New Covenant (Deuteronomy 18:15–19, Jeremiah 31:31–34).

Christ comes as the prophet like Moses (Acts 3:22, 7:37). Shortly after his birth, through the faithful action of his mother, Moses narrowly escapes those who seek to kill newborn boys among the Israelite slaves. Through the faithfulness of Mary and Joseph, Jesus escapes the soldiers sent by Herod to kill the boys of Bethlehem. Moses spends forty years in the wilderness. Jesus prepares for his mission with forty days in the wilderness. Like Moses, who brings the law down from the mountain in the Sermon on the Mount, Jesus proclaims the new law from a mountain. Like Moses through whom God feeds the multitudes of Israel in the wilderness with manna, Jesus miraculously feeds multitudes that have followed him into a wilderness area. However, Jesus is greater than Moses. Whereas Moses feeds the people with manna to preserve their physical life, Jesus promises the bread of life, his flesh which brings spiritual and eternal life. Moses leads Israel in her exodus from Egyptian slavery toward freedom in the promised land, but Jesus leads mankind in a new exodus from slavery to sin and death toward eternal life. Jesus' own death and resurrection is our new exodus of redemption. Jesus claims an authority surpassing that of Moses and the Torah. In his Sermon on the Mount, Jesus proclaims repeatedly, "It was said (in the Law of Moses) but I say to you...." The glory of the Old Covenant given through Moses fades before the light of the new covenant brought by Jesus (2 Corinthians 4:7–11). The new law is written on our hearts by the Holy Spirit given in abundance and without limits by Jesus. Jesus surpasses Moses as prophet, because Jesus is the Son who eternally and intimately knows the Father and who alone can reveal the fullness of the Father (Hebrews 3:1–6, Matthew 11:27, John 1:17–18).

WORD AND WISDOM OF GOD

Jesus' role as revealer is developed not only by his superlative comparison to Moses, but also by recognizing him as the Incarnation of the very Word and Wisdom of God. As Son of the Father, Jesus fully reveals God and his plan for humanity. Whereas the word of the Lord comes to Moses and other prophets, Jesus is the Word itself, revealed in the flesh. According to the prologue of John's Gospel, as Word of God, Jesus in eternity "was God," fully sharing in the divine nature of the Father, and he is at the same time "with God" as the Son and Word who is the expression of the Father (John 1:1–3). In the Old Testament, the "Word of God" could express God's word of creation by which he spoke the world into existence, his prophetic word through which God acts in human history, and the word of the covenant by which he enters into relationship with his people. By referring to Jesus as the Word of God, the fourth Gospel identifies Jesus with God himself in his creative, prophetic, and covenantal action. At the same time, the Greek term for the word *Logos* was widely used in Greek philosophy to describe the divine reason which orders the universe and imparts rationality to human souls. The Word of God revealed to the Jews and that same divine Word discovered by human reason among the Greeks is fully revealed in the Incarnation of that Word, Jesus Christ.

Along with this use of the term, Word, the Old Testament also speaks of the Wisdom of God. Jesus spoke of himself as greater than Solomon, renowned as the wisest of Israel, and used the language of wisdom itself. Rather than calling his disciples to take on the yoke of wisdom, Jesus identifies himself with wisdom and calls them to take on his yoke (Matthew 11:28–30, 12:42; see Sirach 51:23–27). Thus, Saint Paul calls Jesus the Wisdom of God (1 Corinthians 1:24). The book of Hebrews borrows the description of wisdom from the book, Wisdom of Solomon, to describe Jesus as the reflection of the glory of God by whom the world was made and in whom the world is upheld (Hebrews 1:1–3, Wisdom 7:25–26). As Word and Wisdom of God, Jesus fulfills, perfects, and completes the history of prophetic revelation which began with Moses. The climax of Jesus' revelation as divine wisdom is the cross where he reveals the extent of the divine love for mankind. Thus, Saint Paul calls us to glory in the wisdom of the cross (1 Corinthians 1:20–25, 2:1–2).

NEW HIGH PRIEST IN THE ORDER OF MELCHIZEDEK

At his last supper with the Apostles, Jesus speaks in the priestly language of sacrifice as he gives his Body and Blood, which is offered for us. Previously, he enacted a prophetic sign of judgment on the temple by overthrowing the money changers, recalling the prophecy of a new temple that will be a house of prayer for all nations and speaking of his own body as the new temple that would be destroyed and raised again in three days. Throughout his ministry, Jesus bestows the priestly blessings of healing and forgiveness on those who put their faith in him. However, despite his priestly claims and actions, there is a major obstacle to Jewish recognition of Jesus as a priest. He is not a descendent of Aaron nor a member of the priestly family of Levites. How then can Jesus fulfill the Old Testament priesthood? The Christian understanding of Jesus as high priest is rooted in the messianic prophecies of Psalm 110. This Psalm speaks of the Messiah as both anointed king and priest, a priest in the order of Melchizedek. Melchizedek is the first priest mentioned in the Old Testament. Long before Aaron or the Levites were made priests under Moses, their forefather Abraham gave an offering to the mysterious priest Melchizedek, king of Salem (Genesis 14:18). This royal priest offered a sacrifice of bread and wine. The book of Hebrews speaks of Jesus as the new high priest according to the order of Melchizedek, a priesthood chronologically antecedent and thus superior to that of the Levites, a priesthood not based upon genealogy but upon an eternal promise (Hebrews 7:1–17). Jesus fulfills the promise of God to bring salvation from sin in a new and eternal covenant through an eternal priesthood. As the divine Son who fully shares our human nature but without sin, Christ offers the definitive sacrifice for sin and lives forever to offer priestly intercession in heaven itself (Hebrews 7:20–8:13).

As our one high priest, Jesus gives all members of his church a share in his priesthood through baptism into the new priestly people of God. The baptized offer their lives in a spiritual sacrifice of praise and service to God. Among the baptized, Jesus calls some men into the ministerial priesthood to sacramentally represent him by offering that eucharistic sacrifice through which we unite ourselves to Jesus' priestly self offering and receive the benefits of his sacrifice.

LAMB OF GOD

Jesus is not only the priest who offers sacrifice; he is the sacrifice which is offered. He is both priest and victim. Jesus said that he came to serve and to offer himself as a ransom for sin (Mark 10:45). At the institution of the Eucharist at the Last Supper, it is his own Body and Blood which he offers. In John's Gospel as well as in the Revelation of John, Jesus is proclaimed as the Lamb of God who takes away the sin of the world (John 1:29, Revelation 5:7–10). Both Saint Peter and Saint Paul refer to Jesus as the lamb sacrificed for our sins (1 Corinthians 5:7, 1 Peter 1:19). Saint Paul speaks of Jesus' death as the sign of God's love for us, a death which justifies, delivers from death, and frees from the power of sin (Romans 5:8–9, 6:1–11). The book of Hebrews contrasts the old sacrifices of bulls and goats that could never cleanse from sin, with the sacrifice of Christ that brings forgiveness and sanctification (Hebrews 10:1–18). In a number of places throughout the New Testament, the "song of the suffering servant" from Isaiah 53 is interpreted as describing Jesus as the one who was wounded for our iniquities and by whose stripes we are healed (Acts 8:32–35, 1 Peter 2:21–25). The sacrifice of Jesus, as both priest and victim, completes and perfects and fulfills all sacrifices. It is the Father's gift to us and Jesus' gift on our behalf to the Father. In the Holy Eucharist, we receive this gift from God and, in union with Christ's gift, make a gift of ourselves to God (*CCC* 614).

THE NEW TEMPLE OF GOD

Jesus is not only the priest and the victim of the new and everlasting sacrifice; he is also the temple, the place in which the sacrifice is offered. When the Samaritan woman asks Jesus in which city sacrifice was to be offered, he deflects her question and speaks of a future worship in Spirit and in Truth (John 4:19–24). Although his opponents accuse him of claiming he would destroy and rebuild the temple in three days, his Apostles clarify that Jesus was speaking of his own body as the temple (Matthew 26:59–63, John 2:18–22). Jesus' body, the Church becomes the new temple of the Holy Spirit in which his members are built together as living stones into a spiritual house where they offer spiritual sacrifice as a nation of priests and kings (1 Peter 2:4–10). Saint Paul frequently speaks of the Church as the body of Christ and temple of the Spirit. As members of Christ's body, we live in him as the living temple of the Holy Spirit (1 Corinthians 3:16–17). Saint Paul further describes Jesus' sacrificial death in a word that is variously translated as expiation, propitiation, or atonement but can literally be translated as the "mercy seat" (Romans 3:25). The mercy seat was the place of atonement above the ark, where the high priest sprinkled blood within the innermost court of the Jewish temple. Jesus becomes by his sacrifice this new place of atonement where a new people made up of both Jew and gentile will offer throughout the world an unceasing sacrifice of prayer and praise through the offering of bread and wine, which recalls and makes truly present that one sacrifice for sin in which Jesus is priest, victim, and temple.

Royal Son of David

The two genealogies of Jesus in the Gospels both list King David as his ancestor (Matthew 1:6, Luke 3:31). According to tradition, both Joseph and Mary were descendents of David. As his legal father, Saint Joseph makes Jesus a legitimate heir to the Davidic throne, and Mary, as his true mother, makes him a biological descendent of David. God promised through the prophet Samuel that one of David's descendents would rule over an everlasting kingdom (2 Samuel 7:12–16). From this promise springs the messianic hope of a future "shoot" from the branch of David, a messianic shepherd-king who will gather exiled Israel and liberate her from her enemies, reestablishing the Davidic kingdom centered on Mount Zion where even the gentiles will come to be gathered into God's people (Isaiah 11:1; Jeremiah 23:5, 33:15; Ezekiel 34:23, 37:24). At Jesus' birth, he is announced by angels and recognized by gentile magi, Jewish seers, and simple shepherds as the promised son of David, born to fulfill these messianic promises (Matthew 1:20–23, 2:1–12; Luke 2:8–10, 25–38).

In his preaching, Jesus announces the arrival of the kingdom of God and shows by his miraculous signs that the messianic kingdom is dawning. At the same time, in the early stages of his public ministry, Jesus shows a certain reticence toward messianic claims. He characteristically refers to himself not as "Christ" and "Son of David," but by the more mysterious title, "Son of Man." He enjoins some of those he healed not to tell others and he silences demons who declare his identity. This reticence on the part of Jesus has been described by some biblical scholars as the "messianic secret." There are a number of reasons why Jesus is not more explicit in proclaiming himself as the Davidic Messiah during his public ministry. The first is to avoid the common misunderstanding of the Davidic Messiah as a political liberator. An explicit messianic claim on Jesus' part would fail to communicate the mystery of his messianic mission to bring liberation from sin and death through the cross. Thus, Jesus speaks of the nature of his kingdom through parables, attempting to slowly initiate his chosen Apostles into that mystery. Further, a public messianic claim by Jesus could bring the early intervention of those in power who viewed messianic claimants as political subversives. Another reason for his seeming reticence to claim his messianic identity is that rather than impose himself on others, Jesus invites them to recognize who he is in an act of faith. Thus, he challenges his Apostles and even his interrogators to recognize him for themselves. Finally, Jesus does not presume to proclaim himself as Messiah, but rather, in humility, he looks to the Father to glorify him and place him on the messianic throne. Jesus humbly fulfills his messianic task by going to the cross and trusts the Father to raise him to the throne at his right hand.

In this trusting dependence on the Father, Jesus repeats a pattern lived out by the first David. Even after the prophet Samuel anointed him as the new chosen king, David did not seize the throne from Saul, even when he had the opportunity to take Saul's life (1 Samuel 26:8–25). Rather, he trusted the divine promise and waited for God to set him on Israel's throne. Likewise, Jesus, the new Son of David, reveals himself as the messianic king by faithfully fulfilling his messianic mission, and God the Father exalts him by raising him from the dead and enthroning him in heaven. Jesus fulfills the Davidic promises by establishing an eternal kingdom that gathers Jew and gentile from every nation into the new heavenly Jerusalem. The Church is the witness to this kingdom and its budding forth on earth. The fullness of the messianic kingdom comes when Jesus, the King of Kings, returns at the end of history in the final judgment.

As Jesus approaches the time for his death and subsequent exaltation by the Father, he is more explicit in his messianic claims, even entering Jerusalem in explicit fulfillment of Old Testament prophecy, riding into the city on a donkey as the messianic king of peace, foretold by Zechariah (9:9–10). On entering the city, Jesus receives the praises of the children in their messianic exclamations, "Blessed is the one who comes in the name of the Lord." After his resurrection, Jesus helps his Apostles to understand that the Messiah came to serve and to suffer before his exaltation to the messianic throne. Now that Christ has been raised and enthroned in heaven as the messianic King, the Apostles boldly proclaim him as the Messiah. The messianic title of 'Christ" becomes so associated with Jesus in the apostolic preaching that it becomes part of his name.

SON OF MAN

The Church Fathers interpreted the title "Son of Man" as expressing the full humanity of Jesus. In the Gospels, Jesus' use of the title conveys the humble estate he has assumed as man. As Son of man, Jesus shares our poverty, having no place of his own to rest his head (Matthew 8:20, Luke 9:58). The Son of Man shows himself a humble friend to all levels of humanity, eating and drinking with sinners (Luke 7:34, 15:2). The prophet Ezekiel uses the title "Son of man" in this sense, expressing his humility and solidarity with those to whom he prophesies. However, the title could also express Ezekiel's authority as the man sent by God as a prophet to warn sinful Israel. Jesus expresses his even greater authority, as one sent by the Father, when he claims that the Son of Man is Lord of the Sabbath who has authority to both heal and to forgive sins on this day of rest (Matthew 12:8, Mark 2:28, Luke 6:5). The Son of Man is not only one who is with humanity, he is the one who also represents humanity by offering himself as a ransom for all (Mark 10:45). Thus, Jesus uses the title, "Son of Man" when he predicts his future suffering and death.

Jesus also uses the title "Son of Man" in a manner that suggests he is more than man when he uses the title to refer to his future exaltation and coming in glory and judgment. When challenged by Caiaphas as to whether he is the Messiah, Jesus replies in the affirmative and tells the high priest that he will see the Son of Man at the right hand of God, coming in glory (Mark 14:62). In this and other passages where he speaks of the future glory of the Son of Man, Jesus does not follow Ezekiel's use of the title, but that of the prophet Daniel. Daniel saw in a vision one "like a Son of Man" coming on the clouds of heaven. This "Son of Man" in Daniel's prophecy is a heavenly representative for God's people who will come from heaven to establish an everlasting kingdom (Daniel 7:13, 27). At least some Jewish writings from the time of Jesus, such as an apocalyptic text pseudonymously attributed to Enoch, followed Daniel in using "Son of Man" to designate a heavenly Messiah. However, the phrase was not widely understood as a messianic title. Thus, Jesus could use this title to express his humanity, and at the same time, in a somewhat veiled way, to identify himself with the

Messiah foreseen by the prophet Daniel, a Messiah sent from heaven with more than human power and authority.

The Gospels recall Jesus' own use of the phrase "Son of Man" as a self-designation, but the title seldom appears as a Christological title used by others in the New Testament. Once the full meaning of the term is revealed by his death and resurrection, other more explicit terms come into use. The glorious "Son of Man" foreseen by Daniel, fulfilled by Jesus' present exaltation and future coming in glory, is better expressed by the title "Lord." His sharing in our human condition as the humble "Son of Man" is elsewhere expressed by referring to Jesus as "our brother" who shares our human nature (Hebrews 2:11). Later, in the history of the Church, the Fathers will return to this title "Son of Man" as a way to designate his true and perfect humanity. Jesus' role as representative man, as the Son of Man who represents all humanity, is expressed and expanded in Saint Paul's exposition of Jesus as the "new Adam."

NEW ADAM

Saint Luke's Gospel implies the link between Jesus and Adam in its genealogy which traces Jesus' ancestry all the way back to Adam (Luke 3:23–38). Saint Paul explicitly contrasts Adam and Jesus in Romans 5 and 1 Corinthians 15. Adam is the head of fallen humanity. His disobedience brings death to humanity and all his posterity suffer the consequences of his sin. By contrast, Jesus is the head of the new redeemed humanity. His obedience brings life, and his posterity—those joined to him by baptism—enjoy the abundance of grace which Jesus bestows. The sentence of death imposed on Adam at the beginning of human history is the harbinger of death's reign over humanity.

The resurrection of Jesus is the first fruits of the future resurrection of the dead at the end of human history. Adam is created in the image of God but fails to glorify God, and the image of God in man is marred by sin. Jesus is the eternal image of the Father, the prototype in whose image man was created. By becoming man, Jesus, the new Adam, restores the image of God to human nature. United to him, human nature is renewed and the glory of God restored in humanity. The contrast between the old Adam and Jesus, the new Adam, is further developed by the Church Fathers. Adam falls by partaking of the forbidden fruit of the tree; Jesus restores humanity by offering himself on the tree of the cross. Adam is defeated by listening to the devil's lies in the garden; Jesus defeats the devil by resisting his temptations in the wilderness. Adam falls through pride; Jesus restores man through humility.

In the context of these reflections on Jesus, the new Adam, the early Church Fathers begin to speak of Mary as the new Eve. Eve cooperates in Adam's disobedience by giving heed to the voice of the serpent; Mary cooperates in Jesus' obedience by giving heed to the voice of the angel. Mary's obedience unties the knot of Eve's disobedience. Eve was the mother of humanity; Mary is mother of redeemed humanity. Together with Mary his mother, Jesus fulfills the prophecy of salvation given at the dawn of human history. In Genesis, when God banishes humankind from the garden, he makes a promise of future liberation: through the seed of woman the serpent's head will be crushed. This promise of the future conquest of Satan, the serpent, is known as the *Protoevangelium*, the first Gospel (Genesis 3:15). This promise includes the mystery of redemptive suffering, for the one who crushes the serpent's head is wounded on the heel. The pronoun varies in the ancient manuscripts, so it is not clear whether it is the woman herself or her seed that is wounded and crushes the serpent's head. In fact, both Jesus and Mary suffer the serpent's bite—Jesus upon the cross, Mary as witness to the cross—and together they crush the serpent's head. This is why Mary is often portrayed in art with a serpent crushed beneath her bare heel. This prophecy relates Jesus, as the promised "seed" of the woman, to a recurring theme in biblical prophecy.

THE SEED

The term "seed" comes up again and again as a continuing thread through the Old Testament which is repeatedly linked to Jesus in the New Testament. Jesus is the "seed of David" (Romans 1:3), the promised descendent who fulfills the promises given to the Davidic line. Jesus' lineage, however, goes further back to even earlier promises of God. God promises Abraham that through his seed, all the nations of the world will be blessed (Genesis 22:17–18). Saint Paul, in commenting on the promise to Abraham, emphasizes that the promise is singular, referring to one seed not many (Galatians 3:16). Jesus is the one seed of Abraham who has come to fulfill the promise, to bring God's blessings to all the nations. That promise goes even further back, all the way to the dawn of human history, to the Protoevangelium, when God promises that the devil will be overthrown by the woman and her seed.

By referring Jesus back to the promise of redemption given at the dawn of creation, the New Testament and Church Fathers highlight the theme of new creation. Jesus as the long awaited seed, the new Adam, restores and heals creation. Those reconciled to God through Christ are a new creation (2 Corinthians 5:17). Some of the messianic prophecies speak of the messianic age as a healing of creation in which nature itself will be restored, man will live at peace with the animals, the land will pour forth abundance, water will spring forth in the wilderness, the deserts will blossom, and the reign of death will be swallowed up in life (Isaiah 11:6–9, 35:1–10, 65:17–25). Jesus dwells in peace with the animals in the wilderness, multiplies food in the desert, and promises rivers of living water to quench the spiritual desert in human hearts. In Jesus' resurrection, death is overcome and at his return, creation will be healed. Jesus is able to heal creation, for he is the Word of the Father by which the world was first created. By his becoming man, the creative word and wisdom of God is revealed as the Son of the Father.

SON OF GOD

Saint Mark's Gospel begins by proclaiming Jesus as the Son of God and reaches its climax in the Roman centurion's exclamation, "Truly this man was God's Son!" (Mark 1:1, 15:39). The Gospels of Matthew, Mark, and Luke recall the voice of God declaring at Jesus' baptism and again at his transfiguration, "This is my beloved Son." At the beginning of their Gospels, both Matthew and Luke record the virgin birth of Jesus; Mary is Jesus' mother but God is his father. Both of these Gospels record Jesus' words of rejoicing over the revelation given to his disciples, whom he describes as little infants. Jesus refers to himself as the only one who can give this revelation to these little ones, because he is the Son of the Father. He alone knows, and he alone can reveal the Father to others (Matthew

11:25–27, Luke 10:21–22). This theme of Jesus' divine sonship pervades John's Gospel. John presents Jesus as the Word of God made flesh who is revealed as the only begotten Son of the Father (John 1:14). Saint Paul, too, speaks of Jesus as the Son, sent by God into the world to be born of woman in order to grant us adoption as Sons through the gift of the Holy Spirit (Galatians 4:4). Saint Paul says the Spirit enables us, as God's adopted children, to cry out to God as "abba" (Galatians 4:6, Romans 8:15). This is the same intimate term with which Jesus addresses God as his father, as recorded in the Gospel of Mark (Mark 14:36). It is an Aramaic term used in reference to one's own father. Jesus incorporates us into his relationship to God, teaching us to pray "Our Father." At the same time, his relationship to God the Father remains unique, as illustrated after his resurrection when he speaks of going to "my Father and to your Father" (John 20:17).

This "Father" language for God and Jesus' own identification as Son of God reflect a dramatic theological shift from the Old Testament. God is rarely addressed or spoken of as Father in the Old Testament. In the entire Old Testament, God is only addressed or spoken of as "Father" about a dozen times. In the New Testament, by contrast, he is called Father well over two hundred times. It is Jesus, the eternal Son of the Father, who sees the face of the Father, who came from the Father, who is able to make God known as Father. The language of sonship is used somewhat more in the Old Testament, but still in a limited way. The entire nation of Israel may be referred to as God's son, adopted by God's gracious choice. Angels are occasionally called sons of God. In a few passages, a king, judge, or other ruler is referred to as a Son of God. According to some Old Testament prophecies and Psalms, the Messiah will be known as God's son. Nevertheless, in the Old Testament, this sonship remains somewhat figurative or metaphorical. The people of Israel, angels, kings, and the Messiah are "like" sons of God. In the New Testament, the term "Son of God" is taken to a much deeper level as a designation for Jesus. He is the eternal and unique Son who shares the very nature, dignity, and authority of God the Father. That is why he shares with the Father the divine identity of Yahweh, the God of Israel and creator of the whole world. With the Father, Jesus the divine Son is enthroned above heaven and earth and worshiped by men and angels (Hebrews 1:1–12). The Son, though in the very form of God, assumes the form of a servant in the Incarnation and in the cross, making himself our brother and sharing our nature, that by his humility, we might be saved and made sons and daughters of God.

Jesus reveals the Father by his life and teaching. The Father affirms Jesus' unique divine sonship at his baptism and transfiguration and confirms Jesus as Son by raising him from the dead. Ascended and glorified at the Father's right hand, Jesus sends the Spirit to reveal Father and Son to us. Thus, through Jesus the Son, we come to know God as Father, Son, and Spirit. The Father and Son language of the New Testament begins to reveal the one God as an eternal communion of love between Father and Son in the Spirit. By baptism in the name of the Trinity, we are united to the Son by the gift of the Holy Spirit, sharing in Jesus' relationship to the Father as children of God.

GOD

While the distinction between Father and Son is usually designated by the New Testament use of the divine title "God" for the Father and the divine title "Lord" for the Son, sometimes the word "God" is applied to Jesus. As Son and Lord, Jesus fully shares in the deity of the Father. Thus, John's Gospel begins by declaring that Jesus, the Word, both is "with God" and "is God." The Gospel climaxes with doubting Thomas' eventual faith-filled words of adoration as he touches the wounds of the risen Jesus, "My Lord and my God!" (John 1:1, 20:28). Jesus is called God several other places in the New Testament, as well. (In some passages, it depends on exactly how the passage is translated and/or punctuated, but a strong case can be made that the following passages directly attribute the title "God" to Jesus: Acts 20:28, Romans 9:5, Titus 2:13, Hebrews 1:8, 2 Peter 1:1. In his relationship to the Father, Jesus is Son of God. In terms of his divine nature, he is God.

BRIDEGROOM

Throughout the New Testament, there are still more titles given to Jesus and further Old Testament types fulfilled by him. Saint Paul says "all" the promises of God are "yes" in Jesus Christ (2 Corinthians 1:20). They all reach their fulfillment in him. The entire history of Israel reaches its goal in Jesus, and through that history, God's plan of salvation for the human race is achieved in Jesus Christ. That is why the book of Revelation takes a passage from Isaiah about the God of Israel as first and last and applies that language to Jesus. Using the first and last letters of the Greek alphabet, Revelation refers to Jesus as the alpha and omega, beginning and end (Isaiah 44:6, 48:12; Revelation 1:8, 21:6, 22:13). We must bring this chapter to an end, however, with a consideration of one final title for Jesus: Jesus is our bridegroom.

In the later prophets of the Old Testament, God is spoken of as the husband of Israel, the husband of a wife who has shown herself unfaithful by breaking the covenant and going after other gods. Here, ancient Israel represents all humanity in our sinful rejection of God's law (Ezekiel 16:1–59; Hosea 1:2, 3:3–5). Yet God's love for humanity is merciful and everlasting, and the prophets speak of a time when God will espouse himself to his bride in an everlasting and unbreakable covenant of spiritual marriage (Ezekiel 16:60–63, Hosea 2:16–25). In the Old Testament, this spousal language for the divine love remains merely metaphorical. Spousal, marital love is a love that is embodied. A husband gives himself body and soul to his wife who receives him and gives herself, so that the two are united in communion as one. According to Saint Paul, this mystery of embodied spousal love in marriage is a sign pointing to the mystery of Jesus' union with his Church (Ephesians 5:30–32). In Jesus Christ, the spousal love of God is embodied and given, so that when it is received, we might be united with him in a loving union imaged by marriage.

Jesus' intention to be our bridegroom is signaled by his first public miracle, changing water into wine at the wedding in Cana. With his mother's urging, Jesus ends up, in a sense, presiding at this wedding banquet as the one who provides the wine. As a foretaste of the coming messianic banquet, this wine he serves surpasses all others in taste and abundance (John 2:1–11). Jesus speaks in parables of his coming kingdom as a wedding banquet, and he refers to his own disciples as friends of the bridegroom (Matthew 22:2–14, 25:1–13; Luke 14:16–24). John the Baptist is compared to the one who plays the role of best man in ancient Jewish weddings (John 3:29). Saint Paul reflects this bridal language, not only when he speaks of marriage as sacramental sign of Jesus' union with the Church (Ephesians 5:30–32), but also when he speaks of the Church as one body with Christ (1 Corinthians 6:15–20) or as a chaste virgin espoused to Christ (2 Corinthians 11:2). It is from these biblical sources that the Church comes to be spoken of as the bride of Christ, and the Old Testament Song of Solomon comes to be read as a symbolic account of the Church or the individual soul in its mystical union with Christ the bridegroom.

Like Jacob, who sought his wife Rachel at a well, Jesus, at Jacob's well, seeks a lost Samaritan woman and offers her living water (Genesis 29:1–14, John 4:4–15). In this way, Jesus, our bridegroom, shows how he lovingly seeks each of us. The divine spousal love for humanity is embodied in the Incarnation of the Son. The Incarnate Son gives himself to his bride through the embodied gift of his body and blood upon the cross. In the water and blood that poured from the pierced heart of Jesus (John 19:34), the Church Fathers saw the grace of baptism and Eucharist which forms the Church. Thus, the Church, the bride of Christ, is born from Jesus' side as he dies on the cross, just as Eve was drawn from the side of sleeping Adam. The bridegroom continues to give himself, his Body, Blood, soul, and divinity, to each member of his bride in the holy Eucharist. When we say, "Amen" to the Body and Blood of Christ, we are like the bride who says, "I do." As we receive our bridegroom, we are united to him and transformed by his love. The life of Jesus to which we turn in the next chapter is best read as a love story, the story of God's radical love for humanity embodied and given through the life, death, and resurrection of our Lord Jesus Christ, Son of God, and Son of Man.

CHAPTER 3
The Life of Jesus

PREEXISTENCE

The story of Jesus' life begins in eternity. That is where the Gospel of John begins his story: "In the beginning was the Word, and the Word was with God and the Word was God" (John 1:1). As eternal Son of the Father, the Word was always with God in eternity. Since the Son fully shares in the divine nature of the Father, the Word was not only "with God"; the Word *was God*. The Son, together with the Father and the Spirit, is one God in the eternal communion of the three Persons. The Son lives in eternity in the heart of the Father (John 1:18). The Son is that divine Word through whom and for whom the world was created (John 1:2, Colossians 1:16, Hebrews 1:2). To make the Fatherhood of God known and to make us into children of the Father, the divine Son was sent from the heart of the Father into the world to be born as man (John 1:10–13, Galatians 4:4–6). In loving obedience to the Father and out of love for us, the divine Son "humbled himself to share our humanity" (*CCC* 526).

BORN OF A VIRGIN

The angel Gabriel appears to a young Jewish virgin in Galilee named Mary and announces to her that the Holy Spirit will overshadow her; she will conceive a child in her womb who will be the Son of God and Son of David. This child will fulfill the messianic promises and establish an everlasting kingdom. Her immediate response is the humble question, "How can this be?" Not only was she not yet wed to her betrothed husband Joseph; according to some ancient traditions, she also had already made a vow of virginity. Thus, the angel seemed to announce an impossibility. Gabriel answers Mary, and his answer stands as a response to all those down through history who have doubted the virginal conception of Jesus, "Nothing will be impossible with God!" (Luke 1:37). It is not by the ordinary course of human procreation but by a miraculous act of God that Jesus is conceived in the womb of the Blessed Virgin Mary without a human father. This miraculous birth exceeds human understanding and fills us with wonder. A Church Council held in Toledo, Spain, in the seventh century expressed it this way: "This virgin birth is neither grasped by reason nor illustrated by example. Were it grasped by reason, it would not be wonderful; were it illustrated by example, it would not be unique." That council went on to marvel at the two births of the Son: "Yet, in him both births are wonderful for he was begotten from the Father without a mother before all ages and in the end of the ages, he was generated from a mother without a father." After hearing the angel's affirmation of God's power to perform the impossible, Mary responds in faith and obedience, uttering her "yes" to her role in God's plan for the redemption of the world. The Church continues to honor and venerate the Blessed Virgin Mary for this response of faith and obedience by which she cooperated in the divine plan. Down through the ages, Catholics have joined Mary's cousin Elizabeth in proclaiming Mary, "Blessed among women" (Luke 1:42).

The virginal conception of Jesus was met with disbelief and mockery from the beginning of the Church's history, so it is no surprise that many today stumble over this miracle. In modern times, some have accused the authors of the New Testament of borrowing from pagan myths of semi-divine children born from the sexual union of gods and mortals. This accusation falters upon closer inspection of the accounts of the virgin birth in the New Testament. The language with which the birth of Jesus is described in Matthew and Luke does not reflect pagan sources but is rather deeply rooted in the language of the Old Testament. The precedents to these accounts are not to be found in pagan myths but in the miraculous births granted to infertile women like Sarah and Hannah in the Old Testament. The God who granted fertility to the infertile in the history of Israel now makes fertile the virginal womb of Mary. Further, the New Testament account differs drastically from pagan myths in that there is nothing like a god assuming human form in order to have relations with a mortal woman, but simply the presence of the Holy Spirit coming upon the faithful virgin. Finally, that which is born of Mary is not some half-divine, half human creature as in pagan myths. Rather, in the womb of Mary, the divine Son unites to himself our human nature so that he becomes human without ceasing to be divine.

The virgin birth is the visible sign of the mystery of the Incarnation, the unity of two natures in one person (*CCC* 496). The one who is born of Mary is the eternal Son of God and thus we venerate Mary as the Mother of God. From the Father, the Son eternally receives his divine nature in which he is one with the Father and the Spirit. He has no need of a human father to bring him into existence for he has existed from eternity as Son of God. In the Incarnation, he has a human mother from whom he receives his human nature and in whose womb he is conceived. As Son of the Father, he is divine; as son of Mary, he becomes human.

The virgin birth shows the "absolute initiative" of God in the Incarnation (*CCC* 503). Man does not save himself. We do not produce the Messiah or the Savior of mankind on our own through normal human procreation. Rather, it is God's doing. God intervenes in the genealogy of human history to give birth to the one who will bring about the salvation and perfection of humanity. The virginal conception of Jesus shows the priority of divine grace in our salvation. Redemption is God's accomplishment, not ours.

Born of a virgin, Jesus represents a new beginning for mankind (*CCC* 503). He is the new Adam. He is not just another child born in the long line of propagation from the first and fallen Adam. Jesus is the head of the new redeemed humanity, a new creation. The Church fathers used the term "recapitulation" to describe the renewal of the human race in the Incarnation (*CCC* 518). Jesus is born as man and lives through the stages of human existence, recapitulating human history in order to restore and renew human nature. This term recapitulation is difficult to translate in English, but it conveys the ideas of repeating and renewing human history by uniting humanity to Christ as its new head. Borrowing from the language of computing, we may describe recapitulation as something like a "reboot." With the virgin birth of Jesus, God has "rebooted" human nature and human history. Here is a fresh start, a new creation, the human "program" rebooted and begun anew without the "virus" of sin. We have the option to live our lives according to the old program, Adam 1.0, with all its faults and defects, or to "upgrade" to Adam 2.0, forming our lives in union with the new Adam, Jesus Christ. This upgrade requires new birth in baptism, a spiritual birth ushered in by Jesus, the first to be conceived by the Holy Spirit.

The virginal birth of Jesus introduces a new form of birth in the new people of God (*CCC* 505). We are not born into the people of God through the usual process of human procreation as it was in the Old Covenant. Those born of Jewish parents, by their natural birth, were members of the chosen people of God, under the Old Covenant. In the New Covenant, all are invited to become members of this new people of God by a spiritual rebirth in baptism. Jesus was conceived by the Holy Spirit in the womb of his mother Mary. We are invited to be born of the Spirit by baptism within the womb of our mother the Church. Christ's birth provides the model for spiritual rebirth in the Church. He who was not born according to the flesh or through human initiative, but by the Spirit, invites us to be born from above as children of God (John 1:13, 3:3–8).

With his virginal conception by the Spirit, Jesus introduces a new form of birth that will characterize the new people of God and that birth also introduces a new form of spiritual fruitfulness. Mary in her virginal gift of herself to the work of the Spirit shows forth the spiritual fruitfulness of virginity within the new people of God (*CCC* 505–506). It is not only through the vocation of marriage that one gives birth to children to increase the Church, but the vocations of celibate priesthood and religious life emulate Mary and Jesus in a spiritual fruitfulness in which their gift of themselves bears fruit in the birth and growth of their spiritual children. The spousal vocation of love may be lived toward the fruitfulness of marriage or in the spiritual fruitfulness of priesthood and religious life.

THE CHILDHOOD OF JESUS AND THE HIDDEN YEARS

We are given very few details about Jesus' childhood in the Gospels, but what we are told is full of significance. His infancy, as his whole life, is accompanied by both great glory and great suffering. In the feast of Epiphany, the Church recalls the visit of the magi to adore the infant king. These pagan seers represent the first of the many gentiles down through history who will come to bow down before Jesus and acknowledge the Messiah of Israel as King and Savior of the whole world. At Epiphany, Jesus is manifested as King of all peoples, but his kingship will come only through the cross. That cross is foreshadowed in the suffering of the innocents, the infant boys slaughtered in Bethlehem by Herod's soldiers, and Jesus' own exile to Egypt, carried to safety in the care of Joseph and Mary. When the holy family returns to Israel, their journey recalls the history of Israel's own exodus from Egypt and foreshadows the coming exodus of Jesus when his death and resurrection will liberate humanity from slavery to sin and lead us to the promised land of heaven.

Back in Nazareth, we are given one glimpse of Jesus' childhood in the story of finding Jesus in the temple. This account, retold by Saint Luke, provides an answer to a question many ask today. "When did Jesus know he was God?" Of course, the divine Son knows himself from eternity, so the question might be better phrased as asking, "In his human consciousness, when did Jesus first become humanly aware of his divine identity?" Jesus' response when Joseph and Mary find him in the temple shows that he is already aware that he is the unique Son of God sent into this world with a mission to fulfill. Mary and Joseph left Jerusalem after celebrating the Passover, thinking Jesus was with others of their extended family. When Jesus does not turn up, they return to Jerusalem, only to find Jesus in the temple amazing the scholars of the Jewish law with his wisdom. When Mary remonstrates with Jesus for the anxiety he caused them, he calmly replies, "Did you not know that I must be in my Father's house?" (Luke 2:49). His answer, as rendered in the Greek of Luke's Gospel, could also be translated as "Did you not know that I must be about my Father's business?" Either way it is translated, Jesus expresses his consciousness of a unique sonship with the God worshiped in the Jewish temple and shows his awareness of his mission received from his divine Father. How could he have this knowledge? In the Incarnation, Jesus assumed a real human mode of knowing through knowledge acquired through learning and experience, but that knowledge was always shaped by his "intimate and immediate" vision of the Father (*CCC* 472–473). Because he sees the Father, Jesus knows himself as God's Son sent into the world and consequently speaks and acts with divine authority. What should surprise us in this story is not that the child Jesus knows himself as Son of God, but that knowing this, he returns home to Nazareth and humbly lives in obedience to Mary and Joseph.

From this one event in Jesus' childhood up to the beginning of his public ministry, we are only told this of Jesus' life: "And he went down with them to Nazareth and was obedient to them" (Luke 2:51). Jesus spends many long years living obediently with Mary and Joseph, working daily in Saint Joseph's carpentry business. This quiet life of family and work is often referred to as the "hidden years" of Jesus' life. But despite how little we know about these years, they are rich in significance for us. By his obedience, Jesus begins the reversal of Adam's disobedience and opens the path for our sanctification through the ordinary duties and events of family life and daily work. "The hidden life at Nazareth allows everyone to enter into fellowship with Jesus by the most ordinary events of daily life" (*CCC* 533). In union with Jesus, we may walk the path of holiness and service through our care for our family members and through the faithful stewardship of our daily work.

BEGINNING OF JESUS' PUBLIC MINISTRY: BAPTISM AND TEMPTATION

John the Baptist's first encounter with Jesus takes place while he is still in the womb of his mother Elizabeth. When the Blessed Virgin Mary, already pregnant with Jesus, goes to visit her expectant kinswoman Elizabeth, Scripture says "the babe leaped in her womb!" (Luke 1:41). As a grown man, John is sent as a prophet to prepare the way for Messiah's advent. As he is preaching in the wilderness, he recognizes Jesus as the Messiah and as the lamb who will take away the sins of the world (John 1:29). John must be shocked when Jesus comes to him for baptism, for he has already declared himself unworthy even to tie the sandal of the coming Messiah. John baptizes him in water, but the coming Messiah will baptize with the Holy Spirit. In fulfillment of his mission, Jesus submits to baptism by John.

Jesus' baptism marks the beginning of his public ministry. At his baptism, Jesus is anointed by the Holy Spirit for his threefold messianic mission as prophet, priest, and king. He was not in need of the Spirit, but received the Spirit on our behalf. Jesus receives the Spirit for us, in order to give the Spirit in fullness to all are united to him by baptism. Toward the end of his public ministry, Jesus speaks of the Holy Spirit, as the helper he will send to his Church after his resurrection (John 16:7). Jesus promises to baptize (immerse) in the Spirit those who believe in him (Acts 1:5, 2:38). Jesus did not need to be baptized for sin, because he was without sin. By his baptism, he identifies himself with us in our sinful condition as the one who will offer himself for our sins. By going down into the waters of baptism, he sanctifies water and makes it the instrument of rebirth in the Spirit through the sacrament of baptism. At Jesus' baptism, the Holy Trinity is manifested: the Son is baptized, the Spirit rests upon him like a dove, and the Father speaks from heaven (*CCC* 536).

Immediately after his baptism, the Spirit leads Jesus into the wilderness where he is tempted by the devil himself (Matthew 4:1–11, Mark 1:12–13, Luke 4:1–13). Jesus as the new Adam reverses the first Adam's disobedience by refusing to give in to the devil's temptations. Jesus' forty days of fasting also recalls the forty years the rebellious Israelites wandered in the wilderness. Where Adam and Israel failed, Jesus succeeds, providing humanity and the new Israel gathered around him, a new path of obedience and faithfulness. In the season of Lent, we enter into forty days of penance in which we turn from our own disobedience and unite ourselves to Jesus in his conquest of sin. The temptations Jesus faces are common to humanity: the desires of the flesh represented by the devil's offer of stones turned to bread to satisfy Jesus' hunger; the pleasures of the world represented by the offer of the kingdoms of the world if

Jesus worships the devil; and the human pride which puts God to the test, portrayed when the devil entices Jesus to test God by throwing himself from the temple. In overcoming these temptations, Jesus provides us with the grace to overcome these same sorts of temptations, "the lust of the flesh, the lust of the eyes and the pride of life" (1 John 2:16). At the same time, these temptations are unique to Jesus in that the devil tempts Jesus to fulfill his messianic mission in a way other than the way of the cross. The devil tempts him to gain the allegiance of the people by a shortcut that avoids the cross. The devil tempts Jesus to show his power through splashy miracles and a spectacular rescue from death at the hands of God's angels rather than abandonment on the cross. That is why later when Peter questions the cross, Jesus says to him, "Get behind me Satan!" (Matthew 16:22–23, Mark 8:32–33). Jesus says no to these temptations and yes to the will of the Father, knowing that it is only through his obedience to the death that he will finally vanquish Satan and free mankind from the devil's grasp. We too will be tempted to avoid the way of the cross, but by the power of the Spirit, we may unite ourselves to Jesus in his obedience to the Father which conquered Satan and delivered us from the power of sin. Jesus returns from the wilderness in the power of the Holy Spirit and begins to proclaim the presence of the kingdom (Luke 4:14, 16–21).

JESUS' PROCLAMATION OF THE KINGDOM

At the center of Jesus' public proclamation is the "kingdom of God," or as it is labeled in Saint Matthew's Gospel, the "kingdom of heaven." Jesus begins his public ministry calling all to repent, for the kingdom of God is near. The kingdom has drawn near with the coming of Jesus Christ, the king. The kingdom of God is not a program, but a person. It is centered in the person of Jesus Christ and that kingdom is budding forth in those disciples gathered around Jesus in his Church. There is a mystery to this kingdom which Jesus reveals through parables. Through these symbolic stories, Jesus teaches about the character of the kingdom and invites his listeners to enter into the kingdom by responding to his message.

A number of parables use the imagery of a seed to describe the kingdom of God. Jesus uses the image of the seed to describe the presence of the kingdom as "now but not yet." The kingdom is not yet here in its fullness but is truly present like a seed that grows and transforms this present world from within (Matthew 13:1–9, 24–32; Mark 4:1–9, 26–32; Luke 8:4–8). The Old Testament prophecies led many Jews of Jesus' day to look for a coming messianic age in which Israel would be liberated from all her enemies, God's judgment would fall upon all evildoers, the faithful would be rewarded, all evils would come to an end, and an Edenic paradise would be restored. This present evil age would come to an end when the Messiah came to usher in the age to come. Jesus' parables of the seed suggest a different time frame. Already in this present age, the new messianic age has dawned. In this midst of this fallen world, the Messiah Jesus has come, like a seed planted in the midst of human history. The redemption of the world and its liberation from evil has already begun with Jesus' arrival. The fullness of the kingdom and the final conquest of death and the devil awaits Jesus' Second Coming. Our task in the meantime is to respond to the seed sown by Jesus the sower, to receive him, to allow that seed to be planted in our hearts that we might become part of the growing and spreading kingdom of God. The final judgment is still in the future. Now is the time to invite all the guests to the messianic banquet (Matthew 22:1–14; Luke 14:15–24). Now is not the time for judgment, but the time in which Jesus offers God's mercy and forgiveness to all. With Jesus' coming, and particularly through his death and resurrection, the kingdom of God, the reign of the Messiah, the age of redemption and liberation is present "now" in the midst of this fallen world—but is "not yet" here in its fullness, until Christ returns to consummate his reign.

A modern biblical scholar, Oscar Cullmann, used the following analogy, based on the Second World War to explain the "now but not yet" character of the kingdom as reflected in Jesus' parables. He compared the first coming of Jesus to the victory of the allied forces at D-Day and the second coming of Jesus to V-Day or victory day at the end of the war in Europe. At D-Day, the allies had established a firm beachhead on enemy territory; they had defeated the might of Hitler's armies, and as time would tell, the war was won. They would continue to progress until Berlin fell in 1945. With the first coming of Jesus, the kingdom of God has established a beachhead in this fallen world, the devil has been defeated, the power of death has been overcome, and we already proclaim Jesus as victor and liberator. But just as World War II continued until the final fall of Germany before we could celebrate V-Day, so we await our final victory when Jesus returns and death and the devil will be no more. Jesus' first coming is D-Day; the kingdom is now. But the kingdom is not yet, as we await V-Day, Jesus' Second Coming. Like faithful soldiers in the Second World War who labored on after D-Day, the Church militant wages spiritual battles against our enemies, sin and Satan, enemies that Jesus has defeated but has not yet eradicated.

Other parables emphasize the joyful gift of the kingdom. All are invited into the kingdom, which is likened to a wonderful banquet. If those who were first invited fail to come, others—the needy and the poor and the sinners—are invited to receive the gift of the kingdom (Matthew 22:8–10; Luke 14:21–23). God joyfully welcomes all into his kingdom like a shepherd joyfully reunited with a lost lamb or a merciful father running to meet his prodigal son returning home (Matthew 18:10–14; Luke 15:3–7, 11–32). The treasure of the kingdom is such that one should sell all that they have to obtain it. It is the hidden treasure, the lost coin, the pearl of great price for which one gladly sells all (Matthew 22:11–14, 25:1–13). While the gift of the kingdom is free, we must let go of all lesser gifts and give ourselves fully and completely to Christ in order to receive his gift. The offer of the kingdom is accompanied by the call to discipleship to all who answer the invitation. It is not enough to simply show up for the banquet for one must be found wearing the proper garments or with the properly prepared lamp. To answer the invitation to the kingdom is to answer the call of the king. Those who would follow the king, must take up the cross and follow him, loving him before all else. All who enter the kingdom are called to faithful service and fruitful stewardship until the king returns.

THE MIRACLES OF JESUS

Jesus not only speaks of the kingdom, but shows its presence by miraculous signs. His miracles of healing are signs, foretold by the prophets, of the messianic age. While John the Baptist had recognized Jesus as the Messiah when he baptized him in the Jordan River, he seems to have become discouraged and doubtful while languishing in prison after Herod arrested him. So John sent some of his disciples to ask Jesus, "Are you the one who is to come (that is, the promised Messiah)?" Jesus replied by recalling the prophetic words of Isaiah and said, "Go tell John what you hear and see: the blind receive their sight and the lame walk; lepers are cleansed and the deaf hear, and the dead are raised up and the poor have good news preached to them" (Matthew 11:2–6, Isaiah 35:5–6). By these miraculous signs, Jesus is showing that he is the promised Messiah and that with his coming, the messianic age is dawning. Particularly in his exorcisms, Jesus shows the presence of the kingdom. By releasing people from demonic oppression, Jesus demonstrates that he has power to bind the devil. The exorcisms performed by Jesus are signs that this present age characterized by Satan's power over fallen sinful humanity is coming to an end and the new age of liberation from evil through God's power and mercy is dawning (Matthew 12:28, Luke 11:20).

Jesus' miracles are also signs that reveal the mystery of his divine identity. By changing water into wine at the wedding at Cana, Jesus begins to show himself as the divine bridegroom who brings the new wine of the Spirit to celebrate the messianic wedding feast (John 2:1–11). His miracles over nature show his divine power as nature's Creator. The manifestation of Jesus' power to still the storm and to walk on the water are particularly noteworthy ways to show his identity with Yahweh who had shown his divine power over the waves when he delivered Israel from Egypt by leading the people through the sea. In the Psalms, divine power is frequently shown by God's power to rescue those threatened by storms at sea, and the Lord is described as coming on the waves to rescue Israel (Psalm 65:8, 89:10, 107:23–32). By his power over nature, Jesus identifies himself with the divine Creator whose saving power was revealed to Israel in the Old Testament. His divine authority is shown by his power over sickness, the forces of nature and even of death.

These miracles reveal Jesus' love and compassion as well as his power. Out of compassion for those who suffer, Jesus acts to alleviate human misery. Jesus heals the sick, liberates the demonically oppressed, multiplies food to feed the hungry multitudes, and raises the dead. These miracles foreshadow the ultimate expression of Jesus' love and compassion when he will bear the sin and suffering of humanity as our savior upon the cross. Healing of the body and food for the stomach relieve temporal sufferings, but do not strike the root of human misery: the problem of sin and death. Thus, Jesus performs these miracles to show his power and authority to deal with the heart of the human predicament by providing forgiveness of sins. The ultimate conquest of human suffering is realized through the death and resurrection of Jesus which brings forgiveness of sin, resurrection from death, and eternal life with God where there will be no more sickness, hunger, or death. The miracles of physical healing Jesus offered to some are visible signs of the spiritual healing he offers to all. His healing of blind eyes assures us of his power to heal our spiritual blindness. By raising the lame, he shows us his power to raise us up to walk in the paths of holy living and service. When Jesus raises the dead, we see his power to bring life to those who are spiritually dead. Jesus multiplies a few loaves and fish to feed a multitude of hungry people as a sign to show foreshadowing—how he will feed multitudes with the bread of life through the Eucharist.

The work Jesus performed in his miracles continues through the Church. The ministry of healing is handed on to the Church in the sacrament of the anointing of the sick, which sometimes brings physical healing and always brings spiritual strength. The charism of healing through prayer has always been present in the Church, especially evident in the lives of many of the saints. The Church also carries on Jesus' compassion for the sick through many ministries of health care and the compassionate practice of medical science on behalf of those who suffer. Jesus' power over the devil is expressed in the rite of baptism and other liturgies of the Church. The Church continues Jesus' ministry of deliverance by offering, when needed, the rite of exorcism to free those possessed by the devil. The concern Jesus showed for the temporal sufferings of mankind when he healed the sick, delivered the possessed, and fed the hungry continues in the Church through her many works of corporal mercy for the poor and suffering.

JESUS' GATHERING OF THE CHURCH

Jesus proclaims the presence of the kingdom in words, demonstrates its presence in signs, and begins to gather a community of disciples who will be the signs and instruments of this kingdom. Jesus inaugurates the Church by proclaiming the kingdom and calling disciples. The Church is the witness and the initial budding forth of the kingdom which will come in its fullness when Christ returns. Jesus gives a structure to the Church by calling the Twelve Apostles. The number twelve recalls the twelve tribes of Israel and points to these Apostles as the twelve fathers of the new Israel, the new people of God, the Church. Among the twelve, Jesus singles out Peter whom he renames the Rock and to whom he gives the keys of the kingdom. By calling and anointing Peter and the twelve, Jesus gives the Church a lasting structure which endures through their successors, the popes and bishops (CCC 551–553, 763–765). As he gathers disciples, Jesus teaches them to pray, handing on the "Our Father" as a model of prayer. Jesus teaches us to pray to God as our father, to forgive others as we are forgiven, and to accept God's will as he did (CCC 2607, 2765–2766). Jesus gives to his disciples a new law. This law both fulfills and surpasses the Law of Moses given in the Old Testament. The new law goes far beyond the external performance of the law and calls for an interior renewal of the heart. At the same time, Jesus gives the grace of the Holy Spirit to fulfill the law (CCC 1965). Jesus' formation of the Church climaxes in the Last Supper with his disciples where he institutes the priesthood and the Eucharist as the lasting memorial of his impending sacrifice (CCC 619–611). In his public ministry, Jesus gathered his Church, gave it its structure, law and prayer, its priesthood and sacrifice. But the Church remained in an embryonic state until it would be born from the heart of Jesus, as the fruit of his life poured out on the cross and manifested to the world by the outpouring of the Spirit on Pentecost (CCC 766–767).

THE TRANSFIGURATION

Before heading to Jerusalem to fulfill the final hour of his mission, Jesus prepares by going up to the mountain to pray, taking with him his three closest disciples, Peter, James, and John. On top of the mountain, these disciples see the manifestation of Jesus' divine glory. As at Jesus baptism, once again, the Holy Trinity is manifested. The Father speaks, the Holy Spirit rests upon them as a luminous cloud, and the Son shines with a dazzling white light. With Jesus appear two figures representing the Old Testament law and prophets whose writings Jesus has come to fulfill. Moses and Elijah speak to Jesus of his coming departure which he will accomplish in Jerusalem (Luke 9:31). The Greek word translated "departure" is literally *exodus*. Moses and Elijah appear to Jesus to speak about the exodus he will soon undergo, an exodus through suffering and death to resurrection. Jesus will be the Passover Lamb who, through his death and resurrection, will lead humanity from slavery to sin, Satan, and death to the Promised Land of eternal life in heaven. The glory with which Jesus shines on the Mount of Transfiguration gives the three disciples a glimpse of the glory of the resurrection. But despite Peter's desire to build a tent and remain on the mountain top, Jesus leads them down from the mountain, for he knows the cross must come before the glory (*CCC* 556).

JESUS ENTERS JERUSALEM IN TRIUMPH AND LEAVES BEARING THE CROSS

While Jesus had formerly spoken of the mystery of his messianic mission in veiled ways through parables, he now openly presents himself as Israel's Messiah. In fulfillment of Zechariah's prophesy of the coming messianic king, he enters Jerusalem riding on a donkey (Zechariah 9:9, Matthew 21:1–9, Mark 11:1–10). Waving palm branches, the crowds welcome him with cries of "Hosanna to the Son of David!" We commemorate the Lord's entrance into Jerusalem and join the crowds in acknowledging Jesus as Messiah each year on Palm Sunday. The crowds welcome Jesus with the messianic acclaim, "Blessed is he who comes in the name of the Lord." We use those same words to acknowledge Jesus coming to us in the Blessed Sacrament at each Mass. The phrase appears in Psalm 118, which speaks of the one who comes in the Lord's name as a rock that is rejected but becomes the cornerstone of a new building (Psalm 118:22, 26; Acts 4:11). While praised and welcomed as he enters Jerusalem, Jesus knows that he must be first rejected before he becomes the cornerstone of the new people of God.

The outer court of the temple had become a place of business where animals could be bought for sacrifice and Roman money could be exchanged for the Jewish coinage which alone could be used in the temple. Jesus enters this area and begins overturning the tables of the coin changers and scattering their animals with a whip, declaring, "You shall not make my Father's house a house of trade!" (John 2:16). Recalling the prophetic words of Isaiah and Jeremiah, Jesus exclaims, "My house shall be called a house of prayer for all nations and you have made it a den of robbers" (Mark 11:17, Isaiah 56:7, Jeremiah 7:11). Jesus' cleansing of the temple is not merely a denunciation of economic injustice within the temple walls, but a prophetic sign of the coming destruction of the temple. Jesus will be the cornerstone of a new and living temple that God will build as a place of prayer gathering people of all nations. This new temple, Jesus' own body, too will undergo destruction, but God will raise it in three days (John 2:19–22).

Jesus' cleansing of the temple is the last straw for Jesus' enemies among the Jewish scribes, Pharisees, and leaders of the temple who have long opposed him. They begin to plan for his arrest. Under Roman law, they cannot put Jesus to death, so they conspire on how to hand him over to the Romans for crucifixion. It is important to note here that Jesus was not rejected by all the Jews of his day, for Jesus, the Apostles, and his many followers were all Jews as well. Many more Jews would be converted after Jesus' death and resurrection. As Saint Peter preached and Saint Paul confirms, it was in ignorance that they crucified Jesus, not knowing he was the Lord of glory (Acts 3:17, 1 Corinthians 2:8). Thus, the *Catechism*, following the teaching of the Second Vatican Council, emphasizes that we must not condemn the Jews of Jesus' day, nor the Jewish people down the ages, with the guilt of Jesus' death (*CCC* 597). If we want to find who is responsible for Jesus' death, we must look in the mirror. Jesus died for sinners according to God's plan of redemption. We who sin are the "authors and ministers of all the sufferings that the divine Savior endured" (*CCC* 598). As Christians who know Jesus' divine identity, we bear a much greater responsibility when we add to his sufferings by our sins. Gentle Saint Francis warns us with stern words, "It is you who have crucified him and crucify him still when you delight in your vices and sins" (*CCC* 598).

Jesus' journey to the cross begins with his agony in the garden of Gethsemani. Scripture speaks sparingly of his agonized prayer (Matthew 26:36–46, Mark 14:32–42, Luke 22:39–46). Unsupported by his disciples who have fallen asleep, Jesus prays three times, "Not my will, but thy will be done." Saint Luke adds the striking detail that his sweat fell to the ground like drops of blood (Luke 22:44). The *Catechism* speaks of his prayer in Gethsemani as the full acceptance of the Father's plan, in his human will with its natural human abhorrence to death and suffering. He gives his assent to his redemptive death, saying yes to the Father with that human will which he assumed and made his own, thereby making it possible for us to return to God by joining our will to his in praying, "Thy will be done"(*CCC* 612, 1009, 2824–2825).

Betrayed by Judas, Jesus is arrested in the garden (Matthew 26:47–27:26; Mark 14:43–15:15; Luke 22:47–23:25; John 18:2–19:16). Interrogated by the High Priest and his council, Jesus confesses himself as the messianic Son of Man while Saint Peter denies him outside in the courtyard. Jesus is taken first before Pontius Pilate, the Roman governor who tries to wash his hands of the whole affair by sending him back to the Jewish king, Herod. But Pilate cannot so easily rid himself of this difficult matter for Herod simply mocks Jesus and sends him back to be judged by Roman law. Pilate has Jesus scourged and again seeks to release him. But the crowds call into question Pilate's loyalty to Caesar if he releases this man who seems to claim an even higher royalty than that of Rome. Pilate literally washes his hands, even as he knowingly condemns an innocent man out of political expediency.

Pilgrims to the Holy Land would later piously follow Jesus' footsteps through Jerusalem where he bore his cross out of the city toward Mount Golgotha where he was crucified. Combining incidents described in Scripture with those remembered by tradition, they marked the spots where he fell, where he comforted his mother, where Simon of Cyrene was forced to help him carry the cross, and other significant moments along the path from his arrest to his final burial. For those unable to get to Palestine, copies of these Stations of the Cross were constructed in medieval Europe, where many more could follow Jesus in his journey to the cross. Eventually, statues or images of these stations would be incorporated within every Catholic Church. Especially during the season of Lent we are invited to pray and meditate upon these Stations of the Cross to increase our love for Jesus, manifested in the sufferings he endured for us. Walking and praying these stations, we unite our own sufferings to his as we learn from him how to bear our own crosses. Jesus' mission, which began in Bethlehem, reaches its goal at the cross.

JESUS' REDEMPTIVE DEATH

Jesus' death for us and for our sins stands at the very center and heart of Christian faith. The ancient creed from the earliest days of the Church, quoted by Saint Paul in his first letter to the Corinthians, says, "Christ died for our sins according to the Scriptures" (1 Corinthians 15:3). Elsewhere in that same epistle, Saint Paul declares, "The message of the cross is foolishness to those who are perishing, but to us who are being saved it is the power of God…we proclaim Christ crucified…Christ the power of God and the wisdom of God…For I resolved to know nothing while I was with you except Jesus Christ, and him crucified" (1:18, 23–24:2). The New Testament speaks of Christ dying "for us" or "for our sins," of giving himself up "for all," "for sins," and even "for me." With Saint Paul, each of us can say, "I live by faith in the Son of God who loved me and gave himself for me" (Galatians 2:20). The cross is the manifestation of divine love for each of us and the divine gift to each of us. The cross at the same time is a great mystery. Scripture uses multiple words to convey this mystery. Tradition has used various images and analogies to elaborate the meaning of the cross, and theologians have developed various theories to explain how the cross saves us. Only such multiple approaches can facilitate our reflection on this multifaceted mystery of redemption. One helpful approach to the mystery of the cross is to consider it under Jesus' three messianic offices as prophet, priest, and king. The early Church fathers emphasized the royal aspect. At the cross, our king, Jesus, defeated our enemies and liberated us from the powers of sin, Satan, and death. Beginning with Saint Anselm, the Middle Ages focused more on the cross as Jesus' priestly sacrifice for our sins. Modern theologians have emphasized the cross as a prophetic revelation of divine love. Following this historical order, we will highlight the insights to be gained from each approach.

THE CROSS AS THE REDEMPTIVE VICTORY OF OUR KING

Saint Paul speaks of the cross as disarming and triumphing over the evil powers which had enslaved us (Colossians 2:15). Saint John speaks of the cross in terms of Jesus' glorious reign. Raised up on the cross, he is glorified and draws all men to himself (John 12:32). The book of Hebrews proclaims that through his death, Jesus destroyed him who had the power of death, the devil, and delivered us from bondage (Hebrews 2:14–15). We echo this victorious note when we proclaim in the Mass, "Dying you destroyed our death." By the mystery of Jesus' death, death is destroyed.

Jesus is the king who delivers us by giving his own life as a ransom or payment of redemption that brings freedom (Mark 10:45, 1 Timothy 2:6). The language of redemption reflects a common practice in the ancient world. By the payment of a "redemption" price, a slave could be freed from his bondage. For ancient Jews, "redemption" had a further significance in that they saw themselves as those redeemed by God's mighty act of liberation in the exodus from Egypt. Redeemed by God from Egyptian slavery, Israel now belonged to God in a special way. With redemption comes new ownership. Jesus' death is the new exodus which has delivered us from our bondage to sin, Satan, and death. With that redemption, Jesus has purchased us by his blood. We have been redeemed by the precious blood of Jesus (1 Peter 1:19) and no longer belong to ourselves but to the one who bought us with a price (1 Corinthians 6:19–20). Redeemed from the evil powers which oppressed us, we are now servants of the king who redeemed us by his blood. But much like the loving Father who welcomed his prodigal son, not as mere servant but as honored son, the king embraces us as his brethren and children with him of his heavenly father.

THE CROSS AS THE ATONING SACRIFICE OF OUR PRIEST AND VICTIM

The biblical language of redemption is accompanied by that of sacrifice. Jesus is the sacrificial lamb. His death not only redeemed us from the evil powers that enslaved us but also reconciled us with God. Sin had broken our relationship with God and we were powerless to restore that relationship on our own. God the Father intervened by providing his Son as the holy priest and the perfect sacrifice which could restore the broken communion between God and humanity. Sacrifice in the Old Testament restored communion. The sacrifices were frequently consummated by consuming a portion of the sacrifice in a meal which symbolized this restored communion with God. Jesus gave a sacrificial interpretation to his own death at the Last Supper when he said his Body would be given and his Blood would be poured out for the forgiveness of sins (Matthew 26:28). In the Eucharist, his sacrifice is completed by a sacrificial meal in Holy Communion.

Jesus offers himself as a sacrifice of expiation which removes our sin and grants us a share in his holiness. It is a sacrifice of reparation which atones for our sins against God. It is a sacrifice of thanksgiving in which Jesus leads humanity and all creation in the praise of the Father. United to his sacrifice in the Eucharist, we receive forgiveness, grow in holiness, and offer ourselves in a sacrifice of thanksgiving and praise to God for his great mercy. The New Testament book of Hebrews develops at length the theology of Jesus as the new high priest who offers his own blood in the heavenly temple to provide the definitive sacrifice for all sins. This is the unique sacrifice which "completes and surpasses all other sacrifices" (CCC 613). It is the love of Christ which confers saving efficacy upon his sacrifice, and it his association with all humanity in the Incarnation which makes possible his sacrifice for all mankind (CCC 616). This sacrifice is God's gift to humanity by which he reconciles us to himself. It becomes our gift to God, offered on our behalf by the Son of God who became man to offer himself as our priest and sacrifice. We are invited to unite ourselves to him and in union with him to offer ourselves in a sacrificial gift to God (CCC 618, Hebrews 13:15).

THE CROSS AS THE PROPHETIC REVELATION OF DIVINE LOVE

God demonstrates his love for us by sending the Son (John 3:16, Romans 5:8). "If God did not spare his own Son, will he not give us all that we truly need?" Saint Paul asks, before confidently answering that "nothing can separate us from the love of God in Christ Jesus" (Romans 8:32, 39). The cross reveals the love of the Father who sent his Son and the love of the Son who gave himself for us. Jesus is the good shepherd who lays down his life for his lambs (John 10:11). We can each say with Saint Paul that Jesus loved "me" and gave himself for "me" (Galatians 2:20). This love manifested at the cross is the very love which is poured into our hearts by the Holy Spirit (Romans 5:5). If we ever doubt God's love in the midst of life's sufferings, we need only meditate on the crucifix to see God's declaration of love for us. Because Jesus Christ is fully divine, his death is a manifestation of divine love poured out for us. At the same time, because Jesus Christ is fully human, his death is also a revelation that teaches us how to live as human beings. The cross becomes the pattern of our lives lived in self giving to God and others. Jesus provides an example of virtue and a pattern to follow as we endure the suffering and difficulties of this life as his disciples (1 Peter 2:21, Philippians 2:5).

THE DESCENT INTO HELL

The Apostles Creed traces Jesus' descent to the grave: "He…was crucified, died and was buried. He descended into hell." Jesus did not descend to the hell of the damned but to the realm of the dead. The word translated "hell" refers literally to the "lower regions" and designates that realm where the righteous and unrighteous souls alike descended. As Jesus' parable about the beggar Lazarus suggests, there was a separation in that spiritual realm between the wicked who already suffered punishment for their sins and the righteous who were comforted for their sufferings (Luke 16:19–31). Even those righteous were not yet in heaven, however, for they were awaiting the Messiah who would redeem them from death and open the doors to heaven for them. Thus, Jesus descends to the "lower parts of the earth" (Ephesians 4:9) and "preaches good news to the dead" (1 Peter 3:18–19, 4:6). As is often portrayed in artistic depictions of the "harrowing of hell," Jesus ascends from the grave accompanied by a great host of those souls he has redeemed and raised with him to heaven.

THE RESURRECTION

Saint Paul was emphatic, "If Christ has not been raised, your faith is in vain" (1 Corinthians 15:14). All the Gospels give witness to the resurrection. A note of historical authenticity in these Gospel accounts is the initial discovery of the empty tomb by women disciples. Women were considered unreliable witnesses in the ancient world and if the account were fictional, they would never have appeared as the initial witnesses. The Gospels also describe the initial disbelief of the Apostles, most notably that of Saint Thomas who insisted on touching the scars of the crucifixion on Jesus' body (John 20:24–29). The resurrection was not the product of wishful thinking on the part of the Apostles but the convincing witness of the risen Lord that transformed their fear and doubt to a courageous faith that led most of them to their deaths as martyrs. The resurrection was much more than a spiritual vision of Jesus' soul. His body was raised leaving behind an empty tomb. The very words used for this event, the Greek words translated as "raised" and "resurrection," imply bodily resurrection. In addition to the appearances to the women disciples, to Peter and the Apostles, and to other disciples described in the Gospels, Saint Paul recorded Christ's appearance to more than five hundred disciples gathered in one place. Most of these, he added, were still alive when he wrote, and we may surmise that some of these were possibly known to the Corinthians to whom Paul wrote (1 Corinthians 15:6). The resurrection of Jesus from the dead is a historical event, witnessed by the empty tomb and the appearances of the risen Lord (*CCC* 639, 643–644). The birth and continuing existence of the Church and the witness of her saints, martyrs, and her many faithful members down through the ages provide an ongoing testimony that Christ is risen, alive, and transforming the lives of those who receive him."Without having seen him we love him, though we do not now see him, we believe in him and rejoice with unutterable and exalted joy" (1 Peter 1:8).

While it was an historical event, the resurrection is at the same time a transcendent event. Jesus is raised to a new form of bodily life, a life in which death is conquered, a life that lasts for eternity. Jesus' body can be touched and seen, he eats food with his disciples, but at the same time his body is not limited by space and he appears when and how he wishes (Luke 24:16–43). His resurrection occurs within history but it also transforms history. His resurrection frees humanity from its bondage to death and raises our human nature to a new form of transformed embodied existence in heaven. In the resurrection, God's human creation is exalted to heaven and thus the Church Fathers sometimes spoke of Sunday as the "eighth" day of creation. Sunday has become our holy day, the new Sabbath, the first day of the week on which Christ was raised as well as the eighth day of creation anticipating the new heavens and earth redeemed and renewed by Christ.

Jesus' prophetic, priestly, and royal mission, which climaxed at the cross, is confirmed and completed by his resurrection from the dead. His prophetic teaching is confirmed by his resurrection. He shows his divine identity by his power over death. His resurrection also reveals to us our future destiny to be raised in him and like him at the end of history in the resurrection of the dead. The priestly sacrifice of Jesus' death is accepted by the Father who exalts him by raising him from the dead. His resurrection is our justification. We are raised with him and in him to a new life of grace. Jesus' royal victory over death is confirmed by his resurrection. Death is conquered and Jesus is exalted to reign.

Ascended, Reigning in the Church, and Coming Again

After forty days teaching and preparing his Apostles following his resurrection, Jesus ascends to heaven. Scripture and the Creed use the language "seated at the right hand of God" to describe Jesus' position of equality and shared rule with God the Father (Colossians 3:1; Hebrews 1:3, 8:1; 1 Peter 3:22). From heaven, Jesus sends the Holy Spirit upon the Church on the day of Pentecost (Acts 2:1–21). He exercises his reign as risen and ascended Lord and continues his prophetic and priestly ministry through the teaching and sanctifying ministry of the Church, his body. He will return in his second advent at the end of history in a very public way, coming in glory with all the angels to consummate his rule. He will come as judge. We do not know the day or the hour of his coming so we must prove ourselves faithful servants and responsible stewards of his gifts until he comes.

Sharing in the Mysteries of the Life of Jesus

Every event in Jesus' life is a mystery upon which we can meditate and in which we may participate. "From the swaddling clothes of his birth to the vinegar of his passion and the shroud of his Resurrection, everything in Jesus' life was a sign of his mystery...His humanity appeared as 'sacrament,' that is, the sign and instrument of his divinity and of the salvation he brings" (*CCC* 515). Each individual event is an expression of his prophetic, priestly, and royal mission. In every event, Jesus teaches us, both revealing God and providing a model for us to follow as true man. In each event, Jesus offers himself as a priest and sacrifice for our redemption. There is some saving and transforming grace or virtue which we may receive from each moment in his life. In each event, Jesus is bringing the kingdom to its realization, restoring and renewing humanity in the kingdom of God (*CCC* 516–518). We are to meditate upon each mystery and learn from it. We are to receive from each mystery the grace that it brings. We are to unite ourselves to Jesus in each mystery of his life (*CCC* 519–521).

The Church provides us with a number of ways to share in the mysteries of Jesus' life. First of all, we may daily reflect on a short reading from the Gospels, either as read at Mass or in our own private reading. Each short excerpt from the Gospels is a rich and deep spiritual nugget for us to mine in our prayer and meditation. The daily recitation of the rosary leads us through meditation on the joyful, luminous, sorrowful, and glorious mysteries of Jesus' life. Accompanied by Mary and with the help of her intercessions, we spend each decade of "Hail Marys" meditating on one particular mystery, asking God to help us imitate what each mystery contains and to obtain what it promises. Above all, in the liturgical worship of the Church, we commune with Jesus in his mysteries. The liturgical calendar of the Church guides us in a particular way through the mysteries of Jesus' life. We begin the Church year in advent both remembering the long preparation for Christ's first advent in the Old Covenant and preparing ourselves for his second advent. At Christmas we celebrate the mystery of the Incarnation and the wonder of his virgin birth, followed by the manifestation of his glory at Epiphany. Later in the Church Year, Lent gives us time to join Christ in the wilderness, to hear his call to discipleship in his public ministry, and to follow him as he prepared for the cross. Holy Week invites us to enter day by day into the mysteries of Passion or Palm Sunday, Holy Thursday, Good Friday, Holy Saturday, and Blessed Easter Sunday. In the liturgical celebration of each mystery, we are invited to draw near with faith and love to unite ourselves to the life of Jesus. The mysteries of Jesus' life draw us into the mystery of his Person, a deep mystery which we will contemplate, with some help from the Church Fathers, in the next chapter.

CHAPTER 4

The Person of Christ in the Teaching of the Church Fathers and the Early Ecumenical Councils

FROM THE APOSTLES TO THE FATHERS OF THE CHURCH

A letter written to the Church in Corinth late in the first century by Saint Clement, an early successor to Saint Peter as bishop of Rome, explained how the Apostles appointed bishops to hand on the Catholic faith to the next generations. Because of their foundational role in handing on the apostolic faith, we refer to these bishops and other Church leaders from the early centuries as the Fathers of the Church. It was their task to faithfully transmit the apostolic faith, respond to new challenges to that faith and to communicate the truth about Jesus Christ in a new cultural environment. The Holy Spirit used these challenges to lead the fathers of the Church into deeper insights into the mystery of Jesus.

Already, at the close of the first century, the early bishops were forced to correct heretical views of Jesus. Saint Ignatius of Antioch provides an outstanding example of a faithful bishop persuasively battling heresy while at the same time bravely facing persecution. Saint Ignatius was one of the first bishops of the city of Antioch in ancient Syria. After serving as bishop for over forty years and leading his flock through one persecution under the Roman emperor Domitian, Ignatius found himself arrested and facing martyrdom when the emperor Trajan reinstated the death penalty for those Christians who refused to worship the pagan gods. Sometime around the year 110 AD, Ignatius was on his way to Rome in chains. Along the way, this bishop did not neglect his duties as a successor to the Apostles but continued to teach, writing letters to the various cities he passed along the way. These letters included many warnings against Christological heresies. One heretical movement in the second century, known as the Ebionites, denied that Christ was divine. They looked upon Jesus as another Jewish prophet. Against those who denied the deity of Christ, Ignatius emphasized that Christ is God Incarnate. Several times in these letters, he referred to Jesus as "Christ our God." As he headed toward martyrdom, Saint Ignatius prayed to imitate the "passion of God."

It was not the denial of Christ's deity which most threatened the faith of those to whom Ignatius wrote, however, but the denial of his humanity. These early Christians were threatened by a false teaching about Christ known as "docetism." Taken from the Greek word, *dokeo* which means "to seem," these false teachers asserted that Jesus, a divine being, only "seemed" to be human. According to these false teachers, Jesus only appeared to be flesh. Their denial of Christ's true humanity resulted from their embrace of the religious philosophy of Gnosticism. This philosophy derived its name from *gnosis*, the Greek word for wisdom. Gnosticism exalted the spiritual and denigrated the material, rejecting any doctrines that implied the goodness of the material world such as creation, Incarnation, or resurrection of the body. They saw this material world as evil and looked upon Jesus as a being from the spiritual realm, who only appeared to have human flesh, sent to give mystical wisdom that would liberate our souls from the physical bodies in which they were trapped. Ignatius excoriated these false teachers for their refusal to believe that the Eucharist is the flesh of Jesus our Savior who suffered for us. Against them, Ignatius emphasized that Jesus was truly born, truly ate and drank, truly suffered, truly died, and truly rose again from the dead. He chastised them for their belief in a "sham" Incarnation, asking whether the chains in which he was bound were a mere sham. The reality of Jesus' death and resurrection gave Ignatius courage to face his own suffering for the sake of Christ. This brave bishop accused these false teachers of offering the "strange food" of an alien philosophy contrary to the solid food of Christian truth and mixing the name of Jesus, like honey, with their poisonous brew in order to entice unsuspecting Christians. For this reason, in his letters, Ignatius repeatedly called his readers to loyalty to their bishops who keep them safe in the teachings of the Catholic Church, where Jesus Christ is to be found.

When Ignatius and the other early fathers wrote, the threats to the truth about Jesus Christ came largely from outside the Catholic Church. Later, however, threats would emerge within the Church as bishops themselves began to debate the nature of Christ. Such internal debates would lead to the first ecumenical councils devoted to the doctrine of Christ.

THE COUNCIL OF NICAEA: JESUS CHRIST IS FULLY DIVINE.

The Council of Nicaea was convened to address a division in the Church occasioned by the views of Arius, a priest of Alexandria, Egypt. Arius attempted to uphold the unity of God by separating Christ the Word from God the Father. According to Arius, the Father was the one eternal God who at one time made the Word or Logos by which he created the world. The Logos, Incarnate as Jesus Christ, was less than fully divine. God the Father remained the eternal unchanging one who created and redeemed the world through the Logos as his intermediary. This view was popular, for it seemed to protect monotheistic faith in the one God and was consistent with a widely held philosophical perspective which posited a semi-divine Logos as the mediator between God and creation. So many embraced this view, it divided the Church. This division concerned the newly converted emperor Constantine, so he called the bishops to come together and settle the issue. Consequently, the bishops of the Church gathered in the city of Nicaea in 325 AD and the eventual fruit of their deliberations was the Nicene Creed, which we recite at Sunday Mass. The council completely repudiated Arius and fully affirmed the deity of Christ.

In the years following the council, however, the debate continued with a number of bishops, now known as semi-Arians, trying to find some middle ground between Nicaea and the position of Arius. The Christology of Nicaea eventually won the day, largely due to the labors of Saint Athanasius. Athanasius was a deacon at the council of Nicaea, and later, as a bishop, he was a steadfast and persuasive witness for the full deity of Christ. At times, the emperors intervened in the debate, sometimes in favor of the Arians or semi-Arians, and more than once Athanasius found himself exiled for his faith. Athanasius persevered and eventually triumphed, for he understood that our very salvation depended on the deity of Christ.

If Christ is not divine, we are lost, Athanasius argued, for only God can save us. As creatures we are called into existence out of nothingness by God. As sinners we have turned away from God, the source of our existence, back toward nothingness. Corruption and death are the inevitable result of sin. By turning away from God, the source of being, we fall toward the dissolution of death. All creation is affected by this turning away from God. Hence, no mere creature can save us. Thus, if the Christ the Word is created by God, he cannot save us. If the Word by which God first called us into existence was not divine, he could not have given us life. If that Word, now Incarnate for our redemption was not divine, he could not restore us to life. Only if the Word is fully divine, can he raise us from corruption and death to eternal life by making us partakers of the divine.

Thus, the Word must be one in being with the Father. The bishops at Nicaea adopted the formula, "of the same essence" (*homoousios* in Greek). This is a compound word combining the word for "same" (*homo*) with the word for "essence, being, or substance" (*ousia*). The Latin rendering of that term is transliterated in English as "consubstantial," meaning "of the same substance." Jesus Christ is of the same divine essence, substance, or being as God the Father. He is all that God is. As a later creed bearing Athanasius' name said, "What the Father is, the Son is....The Father is uncreated, the Son is uncreated....The Father is eternal, the Son is eternal....The Father is almighty, the Son is almighty." This so-called Athanasian Creed was not actually composed by Athanasius himself but was written by an anonymous Latin author some time around 500. While not written by Athanasius, the creed faithfully continued his confession of the full deity of Christ and serves as a helpful articulation of the Nicene faith.

Some bishops initially opposed Nicaea because the Council used the Greek term, *homoousios* (of the same essence) rather than limiting itself to the language of the Bible. Most eventually came to agree with Athanasius that this word was necessary to uphold the teaching of the Bible. But their criticism reappeared in modern times among those who accused the Church fathers of diluting biblical faith with Greek philosophy. These modern critics asserted that Christian faith was so accommodated to Greek philosophy that the original meaning of Christianity was lost. Rather than a loss, the Catholic perspective looks upon the encounter with Greek culture as a great gain. The Greek language had developed a vocabulary to speak about the reality of things. Greek philosophical terms like essence, nature, and substance provided a vocabulary by which the Church could bear witness to biblical revelation and refute heretical misinterpretations of that revelation. This philosophical language enabled the Church to state with precision that the unity of Christ with God the Father is not a mere poetic metaphor but a statement about reality. It is true not just on some level of subjective religious experience, but on the level of actual reality. Jesus Christ is divine.

The Church fathers borrowed Greek terms and made use of them as a tool to point to the mystery of the divine being of Christ. In so doing, they did not reduce the mystery of Christ to the limits of human language, but rather stretched that language to point to the revealed mystery of Jesus Christ. The error of Arius was to reduce the biblical language about the mystery of Christ to the level of things created and living in time. Thus, when Arius read in Scripture that Christ the Word or Wisdom of God was begotten, he assumed that Christ had a beginning. The Arians claimed that there was a time when Christ was not yet in existence. Against Arius, Athanasius argued that we must not reduce God to the level of our human concepts. We must stretch those concepts to speak of God in his eternal nature. The Son is not begotten or generated in some temporal sense like created things. As the Nicene Creed states the Son is "eternally begotten of the Father." It is not like human generation in which a man becomes a father at some point in time when his son comes into existence. God is eternally Father and in eternity he generates a Son who is his eternal Word and Image. The Father is God, the Son is "God from God," a second divine Person eternally generated by the first divine Person within the unity of the divine being.

The Nicene Creed gives a helpful analogy when it compares the eternal generation of the Son from the Father to the generation of "light from light." If we imagine the Father as an eternal sun, we can envision the Son as the rays eternally generated by that sun (and the Holy Spirit as the light and warmth eternally proceeding from the sun and its rays). Saint Augustine found another analogy to the generation of the Son by reflecting on the human soul as an image of the triune God. He saw the soul's activity of *knowing* as an image of the Father's *generation* of the Word. We generate an idea or mental word in our minds. The mind which generates and the mental word which is generated remain one in being in the unity of the soul. According to this analogy, the Son, as the Word, is the eternal self-expression of the Father. As the full and complete expression of all that the Father is, the Word is his image. Unlike our mental words, which are transitory and unsubstantial, the Word eternally produced by the Father exists substantially in the divine being. The eternal Word and image of the Father is a living Word who can return the Father's love as his Son. In the Incarnation, this eternal Word has been spoken into human history by becoming flesh. The Word reveals the Father to us in his Incarnation. Because he eternally comes from the Father as Word and eternally shares the very divine nature of the Father as Son, Christ reveals God and brings God to us through his humanity.

THE FIRST COUNCIL OF CONSTANTINOPLE: JESUS CHRIST IS FULLY HUMAN.

When the next ecumenical council met in Constantinople in 381, the Nicene faith in the deity of Christ triumphed over Arianism, although it would still take some time for the heresy to completely die out and new versions of the heresy would reemerge from time to time. This council also repudiated those who denied the deity of the Holy Spirit. The Nicene Creed was completed at this council with the addition of those phrases confessing the Holy Spirit as "worshiped and glorified" with the Father and the Son. In addition to these issues, the Church Fathers gathered at Constantinople faced a new Christological heresy, one which denied the full humanity of Christ. A bishop named Apollinarius saw himself as a disciple of Athanasius and wished to fully affirm that the Divine Word became flesh, but he did so by denying that Jesus had a human rational soul. The way Apollinarius saw it, the divine person of the Son took the place of the human mind and soul in the body of Jesus. The Word became flesh by inhabiting a human body. Leading the response against this heresy were three bishops known as the

Cappadocian fathers. Saint Gregory of Nyssa, his brother Saint Basil the Great and their friend Saint Gregory of Nazianzus all came from the region of Cappadocia, now part of modern Turkey. They saw Apollinarianism as akin to the docetic heresy that Ignatius of Antioch had combated. By denying the full and complete humanity of Christ, Apollinarius, denied the reality of the Incarnation. Athanasius had argued against Arius that if Christ is not fully divine, we are not saved. In a similar manner, these Cappadocian fathers argued that if Christ is not fully human we are not saved. Gregory of Nazianzus stated this in his formula, "that which is not assumed, is not healed." The Son heals us by assuming our human nature and uniting it to his divine nature. United to the Son in his Incarnation, humanity receives the healing life of God. For this healing to be complete, Gregory argued, the divine Son must assume all of our human nature, both soul and body. By union with Christ, our human bodies will be saved from death in the resurrection. Even more importantly, our minds and souls are in need of healing from the effects of sin. Thus, it was essential for Christ to assume a complete human nature, both body and soul.

The Second Vatican Council reaffirmed and built on the teaching of the First Council of Constantinople when it emphasized that by assuming our human nature, Jesus dignified humanity, joining himself in a sense to every human person. Having fully assumed our human nature, the divine Son fully shares our human experience, completely redeems our human nature, and fully loves us in a human way: "The Son of God… worked with human hands; he thought with a human mind. He acted with a human will, and with a human heart he loved us" (*CCC* 470).

THE COUNCIL OF EPHESUS: JESUS CHRIST IS ONE PERSON.

With the first two ecumenical councils establishing that Jesus Christ is fully divine and fully human, the question remained as to how these two are joined together. The Church had already rejected one solution to this problem. There was an early heresy called adoptionism, which viewed Jesus as a man who was adopted by the divine Son who came upon him at his baptism, indwelt him through life, departed as he hung on the cross and returned to raise him after death. In this view, there is no real Incarnation but only the indwelling of a man by the divine Son. God does not truly share our human condition. Jesus is different only in degree from many other holy prophets in whom God's presence dwelt. Adoptionism divided the man Jesus from Christ the divine Son. There was no genuine unity of deity and humanity in Christ. This heresy was rejected for its failure to embrace the radical truth of the Incarnation, that God the Son truly became man.

This issue reemerged in the teaching of Nestorius, the Patriarch of Constantinople. He was opposed by Saint Cyril, the patriarch of Alexandria in Egypt. (The bishops of these important cities were given the title of Patriarch.) While the real issue had to do with Christ, Nestorius' sermons on the Blessed Virgin Mary started the controversy. Nestorius was preaching against devotion to Mary as "the Mother of God." In Greek, Mary was called *theotokos,* meaning "God bearer." Nestorius thought this language was inappropriate, for he considered that Mary was only the mother of the *man* Jesus. At most, Nestorius was only willing to refer to Mary as *christotokos*, the "Christ bearer." Saint Cyril saw this for the error it was and vociferously denounced Nestorius. He saw that the issue was a matter of the personal identity of the one who was born of Mary. He who was born of Mary was the divine Son, preexistent as God, now born of Mary as man.

As the debate proceeded, it became clear that despite Nestorius' protestation that he was not an adoptionist, he ended up with a mere conjunction of the man Jesus with the divine Son. This was evident not only in his rejection of the title, "mother of God," but also in his insistence that certain names and titles belong to the man, such as Jesus, servant, and Son of Man, while other names and titles belonged exclusively to the divine Son, such as Son of God, Word, and Lord. Cyril insisted on the long practice of the Church to refer all the names and titles to a single person. The Church believes in one and the same Lord Jesus Christ, Son of God and Son of Man, one person who is both servant and Lord. The language of the Church, beginning with the New Testament itself, had long attributed both human and divine characteristics to the person of Jesus Christ. This sharing of attributes (*communicatio idiomatum* in Latin) had become part of the Christological grammar of Christian faith. By rejecting this language, Nestorius distorted the truth it conveyed.

Under the leadership of Saint Cyril, the bishops of the Church condemned Nestorius at the Council of Ephesus in 431 AD. As with earlier councils, it was a concern for salvation that motivated Cyril. Our salvation is rooted in the mystery of the true unity of God and man in the Incarnation. The Body and Blood of Christ we receive in the Eucharist, Cyril argued, is divine and life-giving because that human flesh is the flesh of the divine Son. The divine Son gives himself to us through his own humanity, which he has assumed and made his own. Without ceasing to be divine, the Son has assumed into the unity of his person a human body and soul through the Incarnation. We receive salvation as a gift of divine life shared with our humanity through the Incarnation and given to us in the sacraments.

Grateful for this salvation, we worship the divine Son as God, united to his humanity. At most, Nestorius could only speak of a sort of co-adoration in which we worship the humanity of Jesus because it is somehow associated with the divine Son who alone is worthy of worship. Nestorius compared the honor given to the humanity of Jesus to the honor given to a statue of the emperor. Against him, Cyril emphasized the Church's long tradition of undivided worship of Jesus Christ, God in the flesh. The unity of the Person of Christ is reflected in the worship we give to Christ truly present in the Blessed Sacrament. In our adoration of the Blessed Sacrament we worship the Body and Blood of the divine Son (*CCC* 1378).

Nestorius spoke about the Incarnation as a conjunction of the divine Word and the human man Jesus, inevitably dividing Christ into two persons. By contrast, Cyril insisted on the one divine Person who had united to his Person the human nature he assumed. This means that there are not two subjects, but only one in Christ. "Christ's humanity has no other subject than the divine person of the Son of God, who assumed it and made it his own, from his conception" (*CCC* 466). This teaching was reinforced later by the fifth ecumenical council, the Second Council of Constantinople (553 AD) which affirmed that it is God the Son, the second Person of the Trinity, who suffers and dies on the cross in the flesh he assumed (*CCC* 468). Nestorius' theology could not embrace the mystery of God who shares our human suffering in the Incarnation. Saint Cyril upheld the mystery of the Incarnation and the cross in which God the Son, in and through his humanity, suffered and died for our redemption.

THE COUNCIL OF CHALCEDON: CHRIST HAS TWO NATURES

The teaching of the first three ecumenical councils about Christ are summarized and completed in the fourth ecumenical council, which met in a city called Chalcedon in 451. This council was called to respond to the teachings of Eutyches, who argued that there were two natures, divine and human before the Incarnation, but only one nature after the Incarnation. Eutyches' view has been called a "monophysite" Christology, joining the Greek word for "one" (*mono*) with the Greek word for "nature" (*physis*). In Eutyches' formulation, the human nature of Jesus was either absorbed or somehow mixed with the divine nature. The Catholic teaching, as articulated by Chalcedon, holds that Christ is not part God and part man nor is he the result of some mixture of divinity and humanity. Rather, without ceasing to be divine, the Son assumed our human nature, becoming truly man while remaining truly God (*CCC* 464, 479). The most significant contributor to the theology of Chalcedon was the bishop of Rome, Pope Saint Leo the Great. Previous popes had sent representatives to the earlier ecumenical councils but their theological contributions were far surpassed by that of Leo at Chalcedon. While not personally present, Leo sent a short treatise on the two natures of Christ, later known as the "Tome of Leo," which provided the basis for the Chalcedonian response to Eutyches. When this Tome was read to the assembled bishops at Chalcedon, they exclaimed, "Peter has spoken through Leo!"

As with the earlier responses to heresy by Athanasius, the Cappadocian fathers and Cyril of Alexandria, Leo's defense of orthodox Christology was motivated by a concern for our salvation. Our salvation requires a savior who is both divine and human. Only a divine savior can reveal the Father, destroy death, deliver us from Satan's power, and make us partakers of the divine. At the same time, we need a human savior who can pay the debt of humanity's sin, endure death in order to conquer death, and ransom humanity from bondage to the devil. As one who is truly divine and truly human, one person in two natures, Jesus Christ is the perfect savior.

The Council of Chalcedon confessed Jesus Christ to be consubstantial (of the same substance) with God the Father in his divine nature and consubstantial (of the same substance) with us in his human nature. The two natures are united in a single person. Contrary to Eutyches, Chalcedon insists that the two natures are united in the person of Christ without change or confusion (mixing). The divine nature is not changed or mixed with the human nature. Without losing his divine nature, the Son is born as man, assuming our human nature into his personal unity. Jesus is truly "the son of God who, without ceasing to be God and Lord, became a man and our brother. What he was he remained, and what he was not he assumed" (*CCC* 469). The human nature is assumed but not absorbed (*CCC* 470). At the same time, while affirming the two natures, Chalcedon also rejected the errors of Nestorius, which would divide the two natures into two persons. For Chalcedon also insisted that the two natures are united in the person of Christ without division or separation. By these four negations "without change or confusion, without division or separation" Chalcedon maintained the distinction of the two natures and their unity in the one person of Christ.

These same four negations were used to speak of the two wills of Christ in the sixth ecumenical council, Constantinople III. This council condemned the heresy of the monothelites, those who claimed that Christ had only one will. Having two natures, Christ has both a divine will and a human will, united in the one person without change or confusion, without division or separation. In assuming our human nature, soul and body, Christ assumed a human will and united that will to his divine will. From eternity, the divine Son has one will with the Father in the unity of the Trinity. In his prayer, "Father not my will, but thy will be done," the Son united his human will to his divine will, showing us the way to genuine human freedom through surrender to the loving will of God. We join in his prayer every time we pray "thy will be done" in the "Our Father," joining our wills to his, in surrender to the will of the Father (*CCC* 475, 2824–2825).

THE FRAMEWORK OF FAITH

The first six ecumenical councils provide a framework in which we can contemplate the mystery of Christ. They do not rationalize or remove that mystery but provide the language of faith by which we can speak of and adore that mystery. These councils provide boundaries around that mystery by excluding the misleading formulations of heretical christologies that lead us away from the truth about Christ. First of all the Council of Nicaea affirms that Christ is fully divine. Any formulation that reduces Christ to anything less than God has lost the truth about him. Nicaea excludes all heresies such as that of the Ebionites which reduce Christ to a mere man and all Arian heresies which make Jesus anything less than fully divine. Having erected a boundary against any denial of Christ's deity, the second ecumenical council, Constantinople I, by condemning Apollinarianism, affirms his full humanity. This boundary excludes all docetic heresies which deny the humanity of Christ as well as all those views like Apollinarianism which view him as something less than fully and completely human. Thus, the first two ecumenical councils hold together the mystery of Christ as fully divine and fully human. The third ecumenical council, the Council of Ephesus, affirms the unity of Christ. It rejects adoptionist views which reduce Jesus to a man, indwelt by the divine Son, and Nestorian views which separate Jesus the man from Christ the Lord. (The modern distinction between the Jesus of history and the Christ of faith often reflects a contemporary form of Nestorius' error.) The Council of Ephesus answers the question, "Who is Christ?" Christ is one eternal divine person who has become man for our salvation. This point is reinforced by the fifth ecumenical council, Constantinople II, which insists that it is one of the Trinity who is crucified for us in his flesh. When we speak of "who" Christ is, we should always speak in the singular and avoid speaking in such a way as to divide Christ into two subjects. The fourth ecumenical council, Chalcedon, answers the question, "What is Christ?" That question must always be answered in the plural, for he is both divine and human. Chalcedon excludes any monophysite (one nature) error which fails to preserve the distinction between the two natures. The teaching of Chalcedon is reinforced by the sixth ecumenical council, Constantinople III, which affirms Christ's human will. Thus, these early councils protect the mystery of Christ as the union of deity and humanity in one Person.

These Christological councils also provide a framework for reading Scripture. Some passages of Scripture refer to the equality and identity of Father and Son (John 1:1, 5:18). They are to be interpreted in light of Nicaea as referring to their unity of nature. The Son is of one being with the Father. Other passages make a distinction between Father and Son (John 5:19–23). These passages reflect the distinction of persons in the holy Trinity. The Son is God, but he is "God from God," the Son eternally generated from the Father. They are one in nature, distinct as Persons. Still other passages speak of Christ as less than the Father (John 14:28). Read in light of the ecumenical councils, these passages refer to Christ in his Incarnation. In his divine nature, he is equal to the Father; in his human nature he is less than the Father. In all these passages, whether they refer to his divine nature or his human nature, we are guided by the councils to recognize the single subject of Christ. It is an error to read Scripture in such as way as to ascribe his human attributes to one person and his divine attributes to another person. There is one Jesus Christ who is both divine and human, Son of God and Son of Man. Some passages refer to the Person of the Son in his human nature and others refer to his divine nature. This framework of faith is an important guide to our reading of Scripture for there are those to this day who repeat the heresies of the past. For example, you will find some new religions and some revisionist theologians taking passages out of the context of this framework of faith and repeating the past mistakes of Arius, Nestorius and others, whose views were long ago rejected by the Church. Guided by the tradition of the Fathers and the magisterial teaching of the early ecumenical councils, we are protected from heretical misreadings of Scripture and directed toward contemplation of the true mystery of Christ.

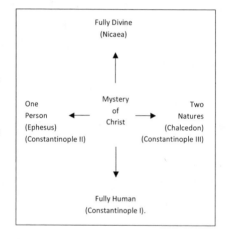

THE FRAMEWORK OF FAITH

Heresies that deny Deity
Christ is not divine (Ebionites)
Christ less than fully divine (Arians, Semi-Arians)

Fully Divine
(Nicaea)

Heresies that deny Unity

Man adopted by God
(Adoptionism)

Divided into two persons
(Nestorius)

One Person (Ephesus) (Constantinople II)

Mystery of Christ

Two Natures (Chalcedon) (Constantinople III)

Heresies that deny Duality

One nature (Monophysite)

One will (Monothelite).

Fully Human
(Constantinople I).

Heresies that Deny Humanity
Christ less than fully human (Apollinarius)
Christ is not human (Doceticism)

NICAEA II: IMAGES OF CHRIST

The seventh ecumenical council, Nicaea II, 787 AD, was called to deal with the issue of images or icons of Christ. A movement had risen within the Church opposed to the use of visual images of Christ and the saints. These images of Christ were known as *icons* (Greek for "image"), and those who opposed them were called iconoclasts. These iconoclasts argued that images of Jesus were idolatrous and forbidden by the Old Testament. The bishops, gathered once again in Nicaea, rejected iconoclasm and reaffirmed the Church's traditional use of images. While the topic of this council may seem to be a discussion of art or liturgy, Nicaea II actually was based upon the Church's understanding of Jesus Christ. The affirmation of images is rooted in the understanding of the Incarnation. The decision at Nicaea II reaffirmed the Christological teachings of the first six ecumenical councils and was based upon the refutation of the heresies they rejected. According to this council, the Church's use of artistic representations of Christ confirmed that the Incarnation was real, not imaginary. The invisible God was truly revealed through the visible humanity of Christ (*CCC* 1160).

The affirmation of images was first of all based on the teaching of the first two ecumenical councils, which confessed Christ's true deity and humanity. If Jesus is truly divine, Incarnate in the flesh as man, this means that God has imaged himself. The formerly unseen God has now made himself visible in the human face of Jesus. In the Old Covenant, images of God were forbidden. God revealed himself as the transcendent God, above any created thing. Any attempt to depict God would reduce him to the level of that which is created and deny his transcendence. In the New Covenant, however, everything is changed by the Incarnation. Since Christ is divine, then God has imaged himself by coming in the flesh. As Saint John of Damascus wrote, "Previously, God, who has neither a body nor a face, absolutely could not be represented by an image. But now that he has made himself visible in the flesh…I can make an image of what I have seen of God…and contemplate the glory of the Lord, his face unveiled" (*CCC* 1159). To continue the Old Testament prohibition of images would be a denial that Jesus Christ is divine and has made God visible. To forbid images of Jesus would seem to be a form of docetism.

The Old Testament prohibition of image "worship" is not abrogated. The images of Jesus are honored and venerated, not worshiped (*CCC* 2132). They are intended for our inspiration, education and contemplation. God did not reveal himself by words alone, but by becoming man, revealed himself to human eyes. Thus, we can learn from the revelation of God in the Incarnation of his Son, not only by reading about him, but also by meditating on pictorial representations of his Incarnation. Some would argue that we should not even venerate these images for they only show the human body of Christ, but such an argument is clearly Nestorian in outlook, separating the divine Son from his human nature. We honor the divine Son, visible through the human flesh he assumed and to which he is united. Because that flesh is assumed and not absorbed by the divine nature, his humanity may be pictorially represented. Thus, the Christological teachings of the first ecumenical councils were reaffirmed by the veneration of images of Christ.

The saving power of the Incarnation which makes us partakers of the divine through union with Christ, also justifies veneration of images of Mary and the saints as well. As Christ reflects God in his human appearance, Mary and the saints reflect Christ in their human natures transformed by grace. By meditating on the images of Christ, his mother and the saints, we are drawn through the image to the reality it signifies, that by contemplating that reality we too might be transformed into living images or icons of Christ (*CCC* 1161).

This issue later re-emerged with the iconoclasm of the Protestant reformers in the sixteenth century. The Catholic Church reaffirmed the traditional teaching of Nicaea II at the Council of Trent. This divergence between Catholics and Protestants is most apparent in the crosses displayed in our Churches. Unlike the empty crosses in most Protestant Churches, Catholics portray the corpus or body of Christ hanging upon the cross. The crucifix serves as a continual visible reminder of the love of God expressed by the passion and death of Christ upon the cross. It is not a denial of the resurrection as some Protestants allege, for every Mass celebrates the resurrection of Christ. It is precisely because Christ is risen that he is able to bring to each of us the fruits of his redemptive death and draw us into union with his death that brings life. Seeing Jesus upon the cross reminds us that we must first bear our own cross if we wish to follow him and share in his resurrection. Contemplating the suffering Christ, we are invited to unite our own suffering to his redemptive suffering. Upon that cross, the divine Son bore the sins and suffering of the world and offered that suffering in a sacrifice of love.

We learn much about Jesus from reading the Gospels and studying the teachings of the Church, but we can also learn much from simply gazing upon his image on the crucifix. There is a story that Saint Thomas Aquinas, the greatest theologian of the Dominicans, went to visit his contemporary, Saint Bonaventure, the greatest theologian of the Franciscan order. Thomas was impressed by the writings of Bonaventure and went to visit the Franciscan in his cell, hoping to see his library to discover the source of his great wisdom. Upon entering Bonaventure's cell, however, there were no books to be found, only a crucifix hanging upon the wall. Saint Bonaventure took down the crucifix, lovingly kissed the feet of Jesus, and told Saint Thomas, "This is the book that has taught me everything." The crucifix can teach us so much, because it reveals the heart of Jesus.

THE SACRED HEART OF JESUS

The image of the Sacred Heart of Jesus has a central place in Catholic devotion, for it conveys in pictorial form the mystery of Christ conveyed by the verbal formulations of the early ecumenical councils. Jesus appeared to Saint Margaret Mary Alacoque and gave her a vision of his heart pierced by thorns and burning with flames of love. By meditating on this image of the Sacred Heart of Jesus, we can grasp the truths about Christ taught by the Church Fathers. Pope Pius XII referred to devotion to the Sacred Heart of Jesus as a summary of the whole Catholic religion.

Devotion to the Sacred Heart reflects Catholic faith in the deity of Christ as it was defined at the Council of Nicaea. The Sacred Heart of Jesus is a revelation of divine love. Jesus' heart expresses the love of God for us. In his heart we see the love of God visibly, concretely, tangibly expressed in a human way. We venerate this image as an image of divine love. Our veneration of the image leads us beyond the image to worship of the heart of Jesus as the heart of God. This heart reveals the infinite depths of God's love for humanity (CCC 478).

Devotion to the sacred heart is also based on Catholic faith in the true humanity of Jesus affirmed at Constantinople I. The image portrays a real human heart. God the Son truly became man. In the sacred heart of Jesus, the divine love is expressed through human love. The divine Son assumed a full and complete human nature, soul and body, human will and human heart. In Jesus Christ, the divine Son made man, God loves us in a human way. He loves us with human emotion. The heart burns with desire for the redemption of mankind. He loves us with a suffering love. God who in his divine nature transcends the suffering and pain of created reality, by Incarnation, enters into his creation and the pain and suffering of fallen humanity. The divine Son enters into and bears our pains, transforms suffering into the sacrifice of redemptive love. The Sacred Heart portrays the suffering that heart endured upon the cross but that suffering was not just physical pain but the pain of unquenchable love poured out upon a world of humanity which often fails to acknowledge his love.

Devotion to the Sacred Heart is rooted in the teaching of the Councils of Ephesus and Chalcedon on the two natures of Christ united in one person. This divine eternal love of the heart of God and the suffering love of his human heart are united in a single person. It is one person, Jesus Christ, who as eternal Son of the Father, expresses the divine love and this same person who having been born of Mary, now loves us with a human heart. The two loves are united in one person. The human heart cannot be separated from the divine person to whom it belongs. The divine love of the eternal Son of God beats in a human heart. That heart is not absorbed into the divine so that Christ no longer loves us in a human way. Forever through eternity, the divine love is expressed through the sacred human heart of the Son of God, Jesus Christ. As we unite our hearts to his, we learn to love as he loves.

CHAPTER 5

The Mission of Jesus Christ in His Church in the Teaching of the Second Vatican Council

JESUS CHRIST IN THE TEACHING OF VATICAN II

The many changes in the Church following Vatican II have led some to question whether the Catholic Church had gone so far as to change her beliefs about Jesus Christ. However, when addressing the many changes in the modern world, Vatican II itself emphasized that beneath all changes there is Christ who is the same yesterday, today, and forever (Hebrews 13:8 cited in *Gaudium et Spes*, 10). It was in this unchanging light of Christ that the bishops gathered for the second Vatican Council sought to illuminate the mission of the Church in the modern world. However, while Christ does not change, the Church does grow in her understanding of Christ and the mission given her by Christ. As the Church contemplates the light of Christ down through the ages, she is guided by the Holy Spirit toward a fuller comprehension of that truth and grows in her understanding of the fullness of truth once given. As the Church contemplates the words of Scripture in the light of tradition, the Lord continues to speak to his bride the Church and through the Church to the world (*Dei Verbum*, 8). So out of the treasury of doctrine and tradition, the Church continues to draw forth new insights, insights however that develop and do not contradict what has come before (*Dignitatis Humanae*, 1). The process we followed in describing the Church's growing comprehension and articulation of the mystery of the person of Christ in the early ecumenical councils continues in the Church to this day. As at Nicaea, Constantinople, Ephesus, and Chalcedon, so at Vatican II the Holy Spirit worked through the bishops in communion with the Pope, gathered in an ecumenical council, to enlighten the path of the Church in her mission to share the good news of Jesus Christ with the world. While those first ecumenical councils were directly focused on the mystery of Christ, Vatican II was focused on the nature and the mission of the Church. The nature and mission of the Church, however, is rooted in Christ. Thus, while their primary subject is the Church, we may also look to the documents of Vatican II and ask what they teach us about Jesus Christ. I do not intend to give anything close to a complete exposition of these documents but simply to highlight, in this final brief chapter, a few points relevant to our understanding of Jesus Christ. Vatican II presents Jesus Christ as the prophet, priest, and king who continues his prophetic, priestly, and royal mission through his Church. We can begin describing the teaching of Vatican II on Christ in terms of these three messianic offices.

JESUS CHRIST THE PROPHET

The Vatican II Constitution on Divine Revelation (*Dei Verbum*) presents Jesus Christ as the mediator and fullness of divine revelation. Divine revelation is the self disclosure of God through which he speaks to humanity and invites us to communion with him in the eternal life of the Trinity. That self-disclosure comes from Christ as the Word and Image of the Father. As God's eternal self-expression, all revelation is mediated through Christ. It is from Christ and through Christ the Word that all revelation of God flows. Christ not only is the mediator of revelation, he is the content and fullness of divine revelation. God's long history of revelation beginning with the knowledge of God to be found in creation, through the first promise of redemption after humanity fell into sin, on through God's history with Israel reaches its culmination with the Incarnation of Christ, God's Word and Son. By his words and deeds and above all in his passion, death and resurrection Christ makes God known and reveals the eternal divine plan for human salvation. Through Christ the innermost life of God as Holy Trinity is made known. The Son reveals the Father and gives the Spirit so that humanity might know God as an eternal communion of love and hear the divine invitation to share in that communion through grace.

This fullness of divine revelation through the Incarnation of Christ is handed on to the Apostles who transmit that truth through Scripture and tradition and the continuing teaching office of the bishops as their successors. The Scriptures, when read in the light of tradition and under the guidance of Church teaching, lead to the knowledge of Christ. All Catholics are exhorted to the frequent reading of Scripture, accompanied by prayer, in order to know Christ. He is the central theme of all the Scriptures. Christ is promised in the Old Testament and revealed in the New. The Apostles handed on the truth of Christ, not only through Scripture but also tradition. In its fullest sense, tradition refers to all that the Church teaches and all that she is. Thus, Tradition describes not only the transmission of doctrines but also the perpetuation of the very life of the Church, handed on by her teaching, worship, and life. Thus, it is not only in the teaching of the Church but in the very life of the Church centered in her sacramental and liturgical worship that the knowledge of Jesus Christ is transmitted from the Apostles down through history to each new generation.

Jesus Christ is not only the mediator and fullness of divine revelation within the Church; he is the universal origin and goal of all truth wherever it may be found. The Vatican II declaration on interreligious dialogue (*Nostra Aetate*) emphasizes that the Church rejects nothing that is true or holy in other religions. For the rays of truth to be found shining in other religions are reflections of the eternal Word and Son, who is the light of wisdom that illumines all men. Humanity is created through Christ the eternal Word. Whatever is true in other religions is a reflection of that ultimate truth by whom we were all created. Christ as the creative Word is the origin of all religious truth; as the Incarnate Word he is the goal toward which all religious truth strives. The partial truths found in other religions are given by God to prepare the way for the fullness of truth given in the Gospel. The rays of truth in each religion ultimately point toward the fullness of truth found in history when the Word was Incarnate, personally revealing God to the world.

The Church enters into dialogue with other religions to promote the common good but that dialogue does not displace the task of proclamation. The Church has been charged by Jesus Christ himself to share the good news with all mankind, as is emphasized by the Vatican II Decree on the Missionary Activity of the Church (*Ad Gentes Divinitus*). The Church is the sacrament of salvation, the sign and instrument of Christ's kingdom, through which the saving mission of the Son is extended to all people. The Catholic claim to a fullness of truth for all peoples which brings to fulfillment those truths found in other religions is not so much a claim about the Catholic Church as it is a witness to the gift of truth given through Jesus Christ. The pluralistic theory of religions views all religions as finding their way the best they can toward the truth of the transcendent God which remains forever beyond our grasp. The good news of Jesus Christ proclaims that God has come to us to reveal himself to all of humanity by making himself known in a personal way through the Incarnation. This revelation is a gift for all peoples, and the Catholic Church bears this gift with the responsibility to proclaim to all the knowledge of God given in Jesus Christ.

The Church gives witness to Christ and proposes the truth of the Gospel without coercion. The example of Christ provides one of the sources for the Vatican II declaration on religious freedom (*Dignitatis Humanae*). Christ is our Lord and Master and yet he came into the world as one humble and meek. With patience he taught his disciples, attracting them by the power of his words and inviting them to respond to his message. He provided miraculous signs to stimulate faith in those who were predisposed to hear his message. Christ did not coerce anyone to follow him but invited faith in his message. He did not call down judgment on those who rejected him but forgave his enemies from the cross. His kingdom was established by his own life poured out on the cross. From the cross he wins hearts and rules by love. His disciples likewise are to spread the truth not by coercion but by truth and love.

The revelation given through Christ and by Christ, not only reveals the fullness of truth about God, it also reveals the fullness of truth about humanity. The Vatican II Pastoral Constitution on the Church in the Modern World (*Gaudium et Spes*) begins with a reflection on the dignity of man as created by God, a dignity reflected in human knowledge, liberty, and conscience. This analysis of the human condition acknowledges both the grandeur and the misery to be found in human experience. For human experience is beset by sin and shadowed by death. It is the fullness of divine revelation in Christ which promises fulfillment to the grand aspirations of humanity, offers healing for human sin and weakness, and provides deliverance from death. As the New Adam and head of the new humanity, Christ restores the dignity of the image of God in human nature. By his Incarnation he has united himself to humanity and by assuming our nature given us an even greater dignity. As the Lamb of God, Christ has atoned for the sins of humanity, reconciling us to God and delivering us from the powers of sin, death, and the devil. His death and resurrection blazed a trail for us to follow. The goods for which human dignity aspires find their fulfillment in Christ. The riddles of sin and death which rob our dignity find their solution in Christ. Christ does not diminish human dignity or freedom but brings light, life, and freedom to humanity. Authentic humanism finds fulfillment in the truth of the human person revealed by Christ.

JESUS CHRIST THE PRIEST

The theme of Jesus Christ's priestly ministry is most thoroughly treated in the Vatican II Constitution on the Sacred Liturgy

(*Sacrosanctum Concilium*). Christ is the priest sent into the world as the divine medicine for the sins of mankind. Uniting in his own Person, deity and humanity, Christ is the perfect priestly mediator. Christ our priest gave himself as the sacrificial victim for our sins. From his sacrifice, the Church is born. The whole Church is a sacrament through whom Christ offers his salvation. Christ continues his priestly ministry through the Church, particularly through the liturgy. He is present in the liturgy in numerous ways. At Mass, Christ is present offering himself through the sacrifice offered by the priest, who acts in the person of Christ. His Body and Blood is present under the appearance of bread and wine. Not only in the Eucharist but in all the sacraments, Christ is present by his power. When anyone is baptized it is Christ who baptizes. When the Scriptures are read at Mass and other liturgies, Christ himself is speaking to us through his Word. Even in the prayers and songs of the Church, Christ is present.

The daily prayer of the Church in the divine office or liturgy of the hours is described as the eternal hymn of heaven brought to earth by the Incarnation. As our priest, Christ took on human flesh, assumed our nature, and through that nature, offered perfect praise to God. He continues that praise through the daily prayers of his members in the Church. The members of the Church, by their daily prayers, join in Christ's eternal song to the Father. In that daily prayer, the Church as bride addresses Christ her bridegroom and united to him as her head, joins in his eternal dialogue with the Father.

Christ is not only present with the Church on earth as she offers her worship; in that worship, the Church is present with Christ in heaven. United to Christ, our worship is carried to heaven where surrounded by angels and saints, Christ our priest presents our offering to the Father, Together with the Father he is adored as the Lamb upon the throne.

JESUS CHRIST THE KING

The Dogmatic Constitution on the Church (*Lumen Gentium*) takes its Latin title from the phrase "Light to the Nations." Jesus Christ is the light to the nations who is sent by the Father to gather people from every nation into the kingdom of God. The Church is his sacrament, the sign and instrument of Christ who unites us to God and unites us to one another. The Father's eternal plan is to gather people from every nation into one new people united to Christ. Christ was sent into the world as man to bring about redemption and inaugurate this new kingdom. The Church is the witness to Christ's kingdom and the budding forth of that kingdom in history. The Church travels like a pilgrim through history: bearing witness to Christ the king; bringing people from every culture into the new people of God; constantly renewing herself to better shine in the world as representatives of Christ's rule; and praying for the coming of Christ's kingdom in its fullness at the end of history.

Christ the king reigns over the Church, the messianic people of God. He continues his prophetic, priestly, and kingly ministry through the Church. Christ rules in his Church through the bishops in communion with the Pope, as successors to the Apostles and Saint Peter. Christ the prophet, priest, and king continues his ministry to the members of the Church through the bishops' threefold ministry of teaching, sanctifying, and governing. In Christ's name, as his ordained and chosen representatives, and with the power and gifts of the

Spirit given by Christ, the bishops continue Christ's threefold ministry. They proclaim the truth of Christ in their teaching and preaching; sanctify us (make us holy) through the administration of the sacraments, and govern the people of God as shepherds. Through their ministry Christ is teaching, sanctifying, and governing his people. The bishops on their part are called to imitate Christ the loving shepherd who humbly serves his flock. The priests also share in this threefold ministry of Christ in their ministry to the parish: teaching and proclaiming God's word, offering the Mass and other sacraments for the sanctification of the people, and guiding the flock they have been called to shepherd. They are assisted by deacons who imitate Christ the servant. Through these ordained ministers, Jesus continues his prophetic, priestly, and royal ministry to his people.

But it is not only the ordained through whom Christ continues his messianic ministry. Every member of the Church is given a share in Jesus' messianic mission through baptism. They are strengthened for that messianic mission by the power of the Holy Spirit given in confirmation and constantly renewed in their mission through the sacrifice of the Mass. At the end of each Mass, we are all sent out on mission. Laity have the particular and essential mission of extending Christ's reign in the secular world. As prophets, the lay faithful give witness to Christ in the world by their words and by their lives. As priests, the lay faithful bring their labors, their concerns, their sufferings as well as the needs and pains of the world in which they live and unite them in prayer to the sacrifice of the Mass. Through this spiritual sacrifice of the laity, the world is consecrated to God. As servants of Christ's kingdom, the laity have a twofold mission. First, every baptized Catholic is called to evangelize, to be a witness to Christ by their lives and their words and to extend Christ's kingdom by sharing the Gospel with others. Second, the laity extend Christ's rule over the secular realm by penetrating all spheres of temporal and secular life with the values of the Gospel and renewing the society according to the will of God. This means that Christ extends his kingdom in the world as the laity live the Gospel and bring its values into all areas of life, including family life, education, work, politics, culture, arts, and media. To do this, of course, each lay Catholic must first allow Christ to rule as king in his or her own heart. While the laity strive to extend Christ's kingdom within this temporal world, those called to vowed religious life remind us that the kingdom of Christ is a heavenly kingdom, ruled by a king for whose love one might sacrifice everything this world has to offer. Together, each in their own way, according to their vocation, the ordained, the laity, and the religious share in Christ's ongoing ministry as prophet, priest, and king. To do this, all are called to become like Jesus.

THE UNIVERSAL CALL TO HOLINESS THROUGH UNION WITH CHRIST

One of the most prominent and well known teachings of Vatican II is the universal call to holiness. All are called to holiness: bishops, priests, religious, and laity as well. What is less well known, however, is how Vatican II presented Jesus Christ as the way to holiness. The Vatican II Constitution on the Church, in its chapter on the universal call to holiness, describes Jesus Christ as the "author and finisher" of our holiness. Christ poured out his life for the Church his bride in order to make her holy. He united the Church to himself as his own body and gave the gift of the Holy Spirit so that the Church might share in the holiness of God. His command applies to every member of the Church, "be perfect as your heavenly Father is perfect." By grace, as a gift, we are justified by Jesus Christ, truly made holy in baptism. But we must hold on to and complete that gift of holiness which we have been given. We grow in holiness, through the gift of grace, by following in the footsteps of Christ, imitating him and uniting ourselves to him, allowing the Holy Spirit to mold us into his image.

Bishops are exhorted to imitate Christ the good shepherd who lay down his life for the sheep. Priests are called to follow the example of Christ the mediator, to offer themselves in union with the sacrifice of the Mass, in humble service to their flock. Deacons should seek to please God as servants, imitating Christ the priest who served. Married couples share in the love of Christ and his bride the Church and are called to be living signs of Christ's sacrificial and fruitful love. Those widowed or single may also imitate Christ's spousal love by their holiness and service to the Church. Those who labor for their living may imitate Christ the carpenter who worked with his hands and forged a path of sanctification through work performed in worship of God and service to others. Those who suffer from sickness, poverty, or persecution can unite themselves to Christ in his sufferings for the salvation of the world. Whatever may be their circumstances or duties in life, by cooperating with divine grace, every member of the Church can grow in holiness through union with Christ.

JESUS CHRIST THE SAVIOR OF THE WORLD

Vatican II reaffirmed Christ as the savior of the world. The Decree on the Missionary Activity of the Church (*Ad Gentes Divinitus*) emphasized that no one is freed from sin by their own power, but every person stands in need of Christ as a model, liberator, and savior. Out of love God sent his Son into the world that those who believe in him might be saved. Christ alone is God Incarnate. He is the Son, eternally born of the Father and one being with the Father in the unity of the Holy Trinity. He was made man for us and for our salvation. Only in Jesus Christ was God fully and personally manifested in the flesh. In Jesus Christ the divine fullness dwells in bodily form. He assumed our nature in order to bring healing, to restore communion with God and as head of the new humanity, to unite all peoples in one body. He accomplished this salvation by offering himself upon the cross and his saving work was completed when the Father raised him from the dead. His death and resurrection is known as the "paschal mystery" because it is the new Passover (or *Pasch*) of humanity from death to life, foreshadowed by the Passover of Israel from slavery to freedom. This paschal mystery, the dying and rising of Jesus Christ, provided for the salvation of the world. Christ founded the Church as the sacrament of salvation. The Church has received the mission of proclaiming God's saving work for all men through the death and resurrection of Jesus. Through the sacraments of the Church we are given the gift of salvation by sharing in the paschal mystery of Jesus' death and resurrection. United to his death, we die to sin, and united to his resurrection, we are born again to new life and the hope of our own resurrection and eternal life.

But what about those who through no fault of their own are ignorant of Christ's Gospel and the Church he founded? Vatican II answered this question as follows: "Since Christ died for all, and since all men are in fact called to one and the same destiny, which is divine, we must hold that Holy Spirit offers to all the possibility of being made partakers, in a way known to God, of the paschal mystery. Every man who is ignorant of the Gospel of Christ and his Church, but seeks the truth and does the will of God in accordance with his understanding of it, can be saved" (*CCC* 1260, citing *Gaudium et Spes* and *Lumen Gentium*). The Church begins with the understanding that Christ died for all. He atoned for the sins of the whole world. He provided the possibility of salvation for all. God offers this salvation to all. He predestines no one to hell, but offers mercy to all who will receive his offer by turning from their sin (*CCC* 1037). This salvation comes by our sharing through faith and sacrament in the paschal mystery of Jesus' saving death and resurrection. But for those who are ignorant of Christ, the Church is sure that in some hidden way, known only to God, the Holy Spirit offers to every person an opportunity to share in the paschal mystery. She bases this teaching on the universal love of God. Because God loves everyone and has provided the way of salvation through the death and resurrection of Christ, he offers to everyone a way of sharing in that death and resurrection. For those who know Jesus Christ is the one sent from God for our salvation, they must receive him by faith and be united to him by baptism. But for those who do not know him, God offers a way to be united to Christ through their response to the secret working of Christ's grace in their hearts and minds. Christ is present to them even through they do not know him, for whatever they know of truth, goodness and love comes from Christ, the light of the world, the Word of the Father, the wisdom that illuminates mankind. Whether that truth comes from their knowledge of the natural moral law, the rays of truth shining in their religious tradition, or the inner light of conscience, that truth ultimately comes from Christ the Word of God in creation and ultimately points toward Christ the Word of God Incarnate in history. Salvation comes only through Jesus Christ, but the opportunity to receive that gift of salvation is offered to every person.

PROCLAIMING CHRIST TO THE WORLD

Since this gift of salvation is offered to all, we might question why the Church and every member of the Church is called to witness for Christ. There are a number of reasons every Catholic is called to proclaim Jesus Christ by their lives and in their words. First of all, Christ himself commanded all members of his body to share the good news of salvation. The command to go forth and preach the Gospel to all people is directed not just to the Apostles and their successors, nor only to the ordained priesthood, but to every baptized member of Christ's body. Second, the Church is missionary in her essential nature. The Church is born from the mission of the Son and anointed by the mission of the Spirit to carry the plan of God forward through history. The Church exists as the sacramental sign and instrument of God's mission to save the world. To fail to proclaim Christ would be for the Church to deny her very essence. Every member of the Church is baptized into her mission and shares in her essential missionary nature. Third, while salvation through Christ is possible in a hidden way even to those who are ignorant of him, it does not mean that all those in that situation have responded to his hidden working. They may await the fuller light and knowledge that comes from the Gospel to say yes to God. Fourth, even if some have already said yes to the hidden grace of Christ, we ought to tell them of Christ that they might know him more explicitly and fully. Fifth, simply out of love for Christ and others, we should be moved to witness for him. He desires to give himself more fully to each and every person. While they may not know it, that which each person searches for and the ultimate answer to their happiness is found in Christ. Out of love, and in a loving manner, we should propose Christ to others as that for which they unknowingly seek in their quest for meaning in life. Sixth and finally, the sheer joy of knowing Christ ought to move us to share him with others. When you find some great joy, you can hardly help yourself from talking about it to others. Jesus Christ is the joy of joys, the incomparable gift of divine love given in a human way. The joy of knowing Jesus should lead us to share him with others.